Faith Stories
FROM WOMEN
IN THE PEWS

Compiled and edited by

Jenny Lang

Faith Stories from women in the pews

© 2021 Jennifer Lang

ISBN 978-0-6450194-1-4

Unless otherwise stated, all scriptural texts in this book are from the New Revised Standard Version Bible, copyright © 1989 National Council of the Churches of Christ in the United States of America. Used by permission. All rights reserved worldwide.

The stories in this collection have been compiled and edited by Jennifer Lang. The stories here are those of the women who contributed them, and Jennifer takes no responsibility for matters of fact or inference.

Enquiries about this publication may be directed to:
Coordinator
Tuggeranong Uniting Church
PO Box 423
Erindale Centre ACT 2903
tucadmin@tuc.org.au

Cover design: Bill Lang

A catalogue record for this book is available from the National Library of Australia

Table of Contents

Joan	Along the road to healing	1
Leonie	Following life's passion	3
Kerry	God lifted me out of a difficult situation	8
Jen	Finding my voice	11
Delia	Life after policing - an unexpected journey	14
Gwyn	Ever evolving faith	17
Enid	Sustained by faith	21
Helen H	Surrounded by loving arms	23
Norma	Called to care	26
Jenny	A grandmother's prayer	30
Dorothy	Don't be afraid to ask faith questions	33
Judy	God's guidance and provision	35
Julie	I believe in miracles	40
Pam	A life lived on three continents	51
Cathy	Faith calls for action	61
Mary M	A Journey with a destination-an adventure with God	64
Robyn W	When God seems close to me	76
Helen E	Persist and listen to God's voice	77
Mary H	My journey so far	79
Maxine	Journeying among another culture	84
Margaret M	On a journey	91

Foreword

It is with great pleasure that I write the foreword to this wonderful collection of Christian women's stories. So often, when women in churches decide to write a book, it is a collection of favourite recipes rather than stories that showcase their exceptional faith and discipleship. While I am certainly not denigrating the worth of recipe collections, for far too long that is the sort of thing women were expected to do, and this reinforced stereotypes about women's faith and place in our churches.

It is clear from *Faith Stories from Women in the Pews* that Christian women are inspired by the stories of their peers, and by sharing their stories, they develop networks and relationships that are far greater than the sum of their parts. Together they become a formidable force for good and for positive change, both in the church community and the wider community beyond it.

I highly recommend this collection of stories that share the vulnerabilities, losses, joys, challenges and brokenness of ordinary women who attend our churches. As Jenny says, they remind us of the disciples' journey with Jesus, and that the ordinary can become the extraordinary and can change the world when a group of people walk together, learn from one another and put their faith into action in the community. I trust you will enjoy reading it as much as I did, and find comfort, inspiration and knowledge in its pages to assist you on your own journey.

Rev Elizabeth Raine
Tuggeranong Uniting Church

Introduction

It was some fifteen years ago, when I was attending a women's retreat at Greenhills Conference Centre with our Tuggeranong church women that the idea for this book was seeded. Our speaker at the time encouraged the women to write their faith story. We've had women's breakfasts for many years where women have shared their faith journeys. So I set myself a bigger goal which I wrote down at the time and that was to pull together a book called faith stories from these Tuggeranong women in the pews. I have been privileged to be in a faith community that has really valued sharing stories and encouraging one another. I had collected a couple of these stories from time to time tucking them aside in my Faith Stories file and every now and then I would get a nudge to get going with it again.

Some of the stories have touched on pain, disappointment, joy, loss, challenges, domestic violence and healing from broken relationships. Just as Jesus journeyed with his disciples so there are significant others in our faith journey and the stories of others encourage us in that journey. With retirement came the opportunity to pull it all together and chase up a few more stories but that was short lived. What was really the impetus to finish was the COVID lockdowns and seeing how we all yearned for connection, relationship and community. As I have read each of the stories there is a consistent journeying theme and I was almost tempted to change the title of the book.

This is a collection of stories from the ordinary women who sit in the pews who tell what God has been doing in their lives. God can do amazing things with the ordinary and as we journey with God in life we discover both ordinary and extraordinary ways that our lives have been touched. These gathered stories will be an encouragement to others that God is not just a distant idea, but a reality that we can embrace in our daily living.

1 Thessalonians 5:11 says

> Therefore encourage one another and build up each other, as indeed you are doing.

1 John 3:18-19 says

> Little children, let us love, not in word or speech, but in truth and action. And by this we will know that we are from the truth and will reassure our hearts before him.

Acknowledgements

I would like to acknowledge two of our story contributors, Joan and Judy, who died several years ago before this was completed and who would have been very pleased to see this book come to fruition. It is with the permission of their spouses that their stories are included.

I would like to dedicate the book to these two women of faith.

Many thanks also to my friend Margaret who has journeyed along with me in this endeavour offering support and encouragement.

I also thank my husband Bill for taking the transcript and working his desk top formatting skills to bring it all to fruition. He has also designed the cover.

Jenny Lang

Along the Road to Healing
Joan's story

Seven years ago, around 1997, at the 8.00 am church service my friend Anne planned a service which was to be conducted by the women in that group. It had a theme of healing and as an example of this one of the women spoke of the hard road to healing after the murder of her sister. It was a memorable morning and I learnt so much. I was about to get more lessons about healing.

Twelve months later, March 1998 my kidneys stopped working. It was caused by a syndrome known as Goodpastures. Slightly ironic as our paddocks were, at the time, bare, the result of a drought. Little is known about the syndrome. It attacks without warning and the effects are usually irreversible. I was suddenly in a frightening world of chemotherapy, constant blood tests and dialysis. My family were very bewildered and scared too. Serious illness had not really touched our family before.

There was an overwhelming flood of love and concern. So many people were praying for me and it worried me that I felt unable to pray for myself. I mentioned this to an old friend and he said that it is OK and just to lie back and rest in the prayers of others. I found this very helpful. I could feel a sense of relief that in my weakness I didn't have to do anything.

Six rocky years have passed. I've had two attempts at a transplant. Both were unsuccessful and I am now off the transplant list. I have dialysis three times a week. If I can book into a dialysis centre, I can travel interstate and have so many times including a visit to Magnetic Island in North Queensland.

Throughout the years I have felt God's love in many ways. I have two gorgeous grandsons who bring me much pleasure. They are totally at ease with the dialysis and are an integral part of my healing as are Ian and my two daughters Lisa and Jacqui and my son in law Paul. They encourage me to be adventurous and gently push me to try harder.

Faith stories from women in the pews

By healing I mean developing an attitude so that I get the best out of the rest of my life. I am trying not to let dialysis overwhelm me so that it spoils the other areas of my life. Throughout the period I have learned that prayers offered to God on my behalf are very powerful and the knowledge that others are praying is a great encouragement. Thank you for your love and continuing support.

I would like to finish with these words of assurance that my friend Anne used at our service. "We are unique and belong to the family of God and of all people, and if we are willing, God, who is for us, gives us the grace to turn from destructiveness in all its forms to new life."

Following life's passion
Leonie's story

I am Leonie married to Peter with a son and daughter of whom we are proud and with all of us confessing Jesus as our Saviour. I was brought up in a Christian home. Church going, faith in Jesus our Saviour and looking after others were what I understood. In my childhood we observed the Christian faith as members of a very local Baptist church (five houses along from where we lived and to which I walked on our wedding day). But the story of my faith begins earlier. My father was a fireman for the steam trains in the railway. Before I was born as the fifth surviving child, my parents attended and were involved in whatever protestant church was in the town they lived in their many railway shifts. I guess I learnt from the conversations that worshipping God was not about the 'flavour' of the church but a relationship with God.

At the Semaphore Park Baptist church, I went to Sunday School and participated with the 300 or so children on the stage for the Sunday School Anniversaries. Like my mother I used to recite poetry and scripture and always at the anniversary. Of the usual 6 celebrations over the two weeks there was always one in which a Salvation Army man attended who would call out as I recited, "Praise the Lord" or "Hallelujah." That man never knew that his outward expression meant more to me than any encouragement of what I was doing. I guess I understood in my childish way that our voice for God, no matter our age can be used to build up others.

Later in Primary School I began to understand that the message taken from Sunday School and the Bible stories was more than, 'here's the goodie, here's the baddie and you should be like the goodie.' Fortunately, one woman heard the call to organise 'Christian Endeavour' and the participation in it for me encapsulated the understanding of seeking to know Jesus more, scripture memory, prayer, living life in the Jesus' way and thus showing God's love to others.

Faith stories from women in the pews

As my siblings were all considerably older and not necessarily in my life at times, I enjoyed attending Christian Camps in primary and high school and the church rallies aimed at our generation. With a second cousin battling lung cancer, I would let him know how these rallies which he was involved in, was part of the shaping of my Christian life. The rallies certainly taught me that Christian expression could just as easily be given in humorous ways as well as the more conventional. One of the leaders at a sailing camp must have challenged my faith and I will always remember him coming over as I quietly cried. I asked him what I had to give to others, and he replied, "Leonie, you have a smile." God speaks and directs our lives in so many ways but not always understood until years later.

Another important part of early life as it impacted my faith and out-working of it was the many occasions, even from Primary School where I showed compassion and desire to assist those who had disabilities or were struggling with issues. From the experiences of the 'Special Class' next to mine led by a Christian teacher and the morning phonic lessons I was asked to give to a struggling child in my class I cared for those who were 'fringe dwellers.' It also developed the desire in me to become a 'Special Class' teacher as it was then called. I also had developed a strong sense of what was just or unjust. As life continued those with disabilities or other needs continued to come my way in whatever venture I took part in or felt God had called me to. In high school I led a group to raise money for sunflower seeds for oil production to assist the income of people in India for example.

In high school I had a close Roman Catholic girlfriend and we understood that we shared the same beliefs no matter the style of worship and sometimes other students would try to put the 'cat among the pigeons' but we were resolute in our shared faith.

I didn't get to teachers' college but became a Psychiatric Nurse – still in the area of assisting the fringe dweller and needy. I often wonder exactly what God had in mind for me there, as much was confusing and not satisfactory really. I can only assume that I was on a journey of steppingstones that has impact on the person I am. I did not always live the life I believed should be led but God places people in our path to help us on the way. It was good that God gave me Kathryn, a Christian in the room next door at the nurses' home who remains close after all these years. Even - or especially - Christians need someone to share their inner thoughts and doubts and joys and Kathryn and I have each other. During the Psych days I was part of a street theatre group, called 'God's Galahs' – another way of expressing faith matters to the world. We went to the mall with our bin of props, and our carpet and entertained those who stopped.

In that time, I also met Peter who was studying at university. I am a person who often understands things in picture language and after one month of 'going with' Peter it was a God experience which I felt, saw and understood, and I knew God was giving His blessing to our relationship. The next day we agreed to marry and did so in the same year. Our young adult church group was important to us with Bible Study, Contemporary Worship we ran and outreach to some of the 'fringe dwellers' who were involved with 'Dominics,' the social group.

In the early days of our year in Glasgow, Scotland (from 2 years after we married) when trying to find a church to attend, we understood the importance of 'belonging.' It was not how we worshipped that was essential but being part of a close group of like-minded friends to share worship, study the Bible, enjoy hospitality and experience fun times. Many of our group became missionaries and church leaders or worked for the poorest folk as doctors in South Africa using their individual God-given talents. Peter and I kept in touch with quite a few and still do with some. I also learnt that a desire to assist doesn't always mean that one is the 'best fit' for the task! I volunteered at a women and girls shelter but in trying to break up an argument the girls turned on me because I couldn't understand them! It was a fair comment considering their strong Glaswegian brogue!

In 1981 we came to Canberra where Peter used his science skills in the Patent Office and we began and brought up our family. Did we choose our first church here? Actually NO! My cousin and family wanted to bring their children up in the church (as opposed to sending them to Sunday School.) As the cousin's wife had a long family history of involvement in the Churches of Christ we joined them in the place they thought they might belong. In a way God honoured our support of the family as we became involved for quite a few years with that church community, worship and friendships. As the children got a bit older, we decided to move to a church in our neighbourhood and so we went to the local school where one part of the Tuggeranong Uniting Church worshipped. Here we were involved in a great community of people and who later also had differing styles of worship in the one church building which was a blessing for us. We had community and belonging but we, like our time of Contemporary Worship in our younger days, valued the ability to worship in less conforming ways.

I wrote earlier of how I gravitated towards those who had disabilities or lived life on the edge of their community. I understood in time that I have a passion for these folk – for the disempowered and oppressed. In Canberra I chose activities that assisted people in this way. For many years I was a volunteer or volunteer-staff with World Vision and was enriched by visiting some African countries including Ethiopia to see the holistic ministry (sustainable development/farming practices, reafforestation, water and sanitation schooling and much more). I taught swimming and ended up teaching children with disabilities. God called me to church activities that somehow ended up with people with these needs. I was a Boys Brigade officer for some years, and we had a relatively large group of boys with particular needs. Through an elderly man I picked up for church I became a friend of the daughter who had a history for most of her life as a drug addict. God gives the passion and he puts people in one's path or he calls one to groups or activities in which our God desires gifts and talents to be used. One of my great joys was working as a teacher's assistant for many years in primary schools and in particular with children with special needs. And what of that desire to become a special class teacher? In my work in schools, I was finally doing what I had wanted to but with less stress than the teachers who are amazing. I believe God honoured that desire to befriend and assist in the schools and in so many other ways.

In the year 2000 what was loosely called 'church group' (Now God Space) began at the invitation of a local drug and alcohol therapeutic community. Tuggeranong Uniting had been involved with this 'rehab' in some ways from its inception. With an initial trial over six weeks Rev Ron Peters, his guitar and two volunteers from the congregation each week arrived with a simple format of some songs, a Bible message and prayer for the clients. I was one who continued as part of the team enjoying our time of interaction with clients as various ones attended. At the time of writing in 2021 I am still involved having seen through the years different ways of conveying the hope of Jesus and many ways of celebrating the message of Christmas in early December with fun and food too of course! It has been yet another way God has used my passion for those on the edge and another amazing personal blessing. I continue to urge 'team Tuggeranong Uniting' not just the God Space team to pray for this ministry we are privileged to be part of and for those clients going out to live in the wider community and who we mostly never see again.

I don't believe I have lived without my generous portion of mistakes and regrets. Christianity and our faith walk is lived out in spite of and sometimes because of the areas in which we err. I have been blessed with a clear understanding of my niche but have had to work at what was at the time God's will for me, rather than doing things just because they fit with that niche. I don't ever want to get to a point where I don't think God has anything else to teach me. Being open to God's will is key to our faith journey. I have been blessed in this life in so many ways amongst and in spite of challenges and I thank God.

Faith stories from women in the pews

God lifted me out of a difficult situation
Kerry's story

My faith journey began during a period of great disruption and personal upheaval in my life. I was in my early 20's and had just been diagnosed with schizophrenia. The illness had immobilised me with fear to the point that I was refusing to go to work, had cut contact with all my friends and really did not even feel safe even in my own home. I was suffering from paranoia and incredibly frightening delusions that seemed so real that I was very reluctant to accept the diagnosis and thought that what I believed was happening was actually real.

Surprisingly, it was at this moment when I had absolutely hit rock bottom that something positive and life changing happened to me. I was looking for spiritual support to give me strength to get through this situation and I'd been looking into a number of religions and spiritual beliefs. None of the religions that I had looked into had resonated with me or rung true, until I went to the Woden Christian bookstore and the salesperson there suggested that I read the Gospels.

I hadn't attended church growing up and had never read the bible before. To be honest I had preconceived notions that Christians were judgemental and self-righteous, and I did not expect to connect with Christian beliefs or thoughts.

I was completely shocked when I read the story of Jesus and found it to be the exact opposite of what I was expecting. The themes of forgiveness, mercy, nonjudgement and humility were very moving to me, and Jesus' life of love and sacrifice was very emotive and affected me very deeply. This seemed to me to be the way that people should treat each other and the type of life we should aspire to lead.

I also had a strong spiritual response to the scriptures as I was reading them. I experienced an overwhelming feeling that God was speaking to me directly through the passages and felt engulfing protection and love surrounding me that alleviated some of the fear and anxiety that I was feeling. I knew that this was the right path for me and felt that I had found my true spiritual home. It was like I had found something I did not realise I had lost.

There were a lot of tough years after the initial diagnosis. I became unemployed due to my illness and was left without a reference after 12 years of work. The lack of references limited my ability to get back into the workforce after my recovery.

I was unsure how to re-enter the workforce when the position as the church administrator became available at my church. My previous employment was in IT support and administration, and I had the skills required, so I decided to apply.

I have now been working as the church administrator for five years and absolutely love serving the church in this capacity. My position allows me to promote Jesus' message in my community, reach out to the people around me, and do something with my life that I feel really makes a difference and has an impact outside of myself. I am able to not only use my professional skills and training, but also work in a caring, interpersonal capacity to help, encourage and nurture those around me. This was an opportunity I had not had in my previous work life and something which makes my job at the church so special and rewarding.

I am now the healthiest and happiest that I have ever been in my life, and the illness is well controlled to the point that I rarely have any problems with it.

I continue to be inspired, encouraged, motivated, and driven by my faith every single day. My spirituality gives my life purpose and inspires me with a feeling of connectedness to God, to the universe and to every person that I come into contact with. I also continue to feel the tangible sense of hope and protection which I encountered that day, for which I am eternally grateful.

I am also eternally grateful to my partner Peter, who stuck with me and cared for me through it all, never gave up on me and accepted me in my faith even though he does not hold the same beliefs.

Faith stories from women in the pews

I am truly blessed.

One of my favourite bible verses is Isaiah 60:1-3 because it beautifully expresses the sense of hope and renewal that I felt when God lifted me out of such a difficult situation:

> *Arise, shine, for your light has come, and the glory of the Lord rises upon you. See, darkness covers the earth and thick darkness is over the peoples, ut the Lord rises upon you and his glory appears over you. Nations will come to your light, and kings to the brightness of your dawn.*

Finding my voice in God's time
Jen's story

I have never been a confident public speaker. For a start I naturally speak way too fast – I use the excuse that I was the fourth out of five children. The other four were all outspoken while I was more reserved. I felt as a child that if I didn't say what I needed to say quickly, I wouldn't get a word in – this may not be the case – but it's my story and I sticking to it.

In school I dreaded the required 3-minute speeches which were part of the English program, and rarely slept well before every 'performance.' The strange thing was that, in my head, I could always come up with lots of good arguments for debates, funny stories for speeches, etc, but when standing in front of the class and teachers, I could hardly speak an understandable word.

Even when part of small team meetings at work over the years, I rarely spoke up – unless really confident of what I had to say – and if someone spoke over me – that was the end of it – I refused to continue.

In some ways, this is still true – although I have gained in confidence somewhat – but if you ask a member of Church Council how often I have given an opinion during a meeting, it's likely that no-one will remember me saying anything.

So, as a very diffident public speaker, I never dreamed that I would ever stand at a pulpit (or on Zoom) leading a service, and even less likely that I would even think I could have anything useful or relevant to say with regards a sermon.

But God had other ideas!!

I have gained in confidence and have been willing to take on responsibilities both in church and secular organisations – provided I wasn't required to speak!!

Faith stories from women in the pews

And then one day, several years ago, I was asked to lead a service for our little local congregation in Tasmania. We had a monthly congregation service, where various members were often asked to take part and share the load. So, when I was asked to contribute to the following Sunday's service, I thought I was being asked to provide one section, maybe a prayer, or a reading. (I was willing to do that much) – but no, I was being asked to prepare and lead the whole service, and 'add some personal touches – we don't know you very well!'

As I usually kept a very low profile, it wasn't surprising that my fellow congregation members felt they didn't know me well.

My initial reaction was fear – but for some reason, I said yes, regardless of my reaction – I regretted that response almost immediately!!

However, I went home, looked up the readings for the following week, and thought about it. I was terrified at the idea of leading a service – I was sure I wouldn't be able to make myself understood – and as for writing a message and delivering it – well, that was beyond my personal abilities, I thought.

But then, a strange thing happened – I thought about the little congregation, which I would be speaking to – and God reminded me that they were my church family – and they loved me – and then God said to me – 'what is the worst that can happen to you?' – I thought about it and realised that they could laugh at me – they might pity me – they might disagree with what I had to say – but that was all that they would do to me – a little humiliation was the worst I would suffer – I wouldn't die – I wouldn't be thrown out – they wouldn't be throwing rotten eggs or tomatoes at me.

That thought put it all in perspective for me, and from that moment, I was able to think much more clearly about what I could or should do.

And God is SO gracious. I had a few little stories I could tell about myself or my life, which I was willing to share, as I had been asked to make it personal. When I looked at the readings for the day, I could see how the stories I had would fit in SO well with those bible readings. So, I did a little homework, used some liturgies from other people, and created a service with the pattern of a reading, a little story, a hymn, another reading, another little story another hymn/song etc. I was able to tie all the readings and stories together. Another week, with different readings would not have worked nearly as well. God had planned it wonderfully – and by using several short stories of my life, I wasn't required to write and read one long (and probably boring sermon).

The service lasted only about 45 minutes – but no-one seemed to care – and I received such encouragement and positive feedback, that I was able to continue to lead services and even to write longer sermons (and hopefully, not too boring). Sometimes, I still need to remember that the people I am speaking to are still my church family, and (hopefully) some of them still love me, and, really, I'm still not going to be killed or kicked out. And that always calms my nerves and helps me to continue. I now find leading services and preaching to be extremely stimulating, and I am also much more aware that what I have to say is God's message to my church family, not my ideas and thoughts, and my continual prayer is that I continue to listen to God and speak out the message God gives me.

Faith stories from women in the pews

Life after policing – an unexpected journey
Delia's story

I grew up in Victoria. My Father was an Irish Catholic immigrant and my mother had been a nurse, then became a podiatrist after being exposed to TB. My parents met in Melbourne and I was the youngest of four. We had no choice in going to Catholic primary school and going to Church in Port Fairy.

I had a lot of resistance to faith as I had been subjected to rulers across my knuckles for being left-handed, and I pretty much left the church when I left home to join the Air Force at 17. I didn't believe in a lot that the church had to say, and I pretty much threw Jesus out with the holy water.

At 22 I joined the Australian Federal Police. Every day I was putting on my shield, my belt, my hat, my boots, my own version of righteousness and was determined to get by in this world under my own strength. When I say strength, I had also started getting into athletics and throwing the discus, shot put and hammer and competing in police games.

In 1994 I went to Alabama to compete in International Police Games and then I travelled up to Canada to watch the Commonwealth Games in Victoria. I stayed in a YWCA and one night I was watching the news. There was a story about the American military going into Haiti to restore democracy, to put President Aristide back in charge.

Strangely, I had this moment when I knew that I was going to go to Haiti. When I got back to Australia and back to the office a circular came out asking for applications to go to Haiti as International Police Monitors. I applied and was selected as part of a contingent of 30 Australian police, there were only three women.

We travelled to Puerto Rico for staging at a US National Guard camp before we went to Port Au Prince. We were in Port Au Prince for a few weeks before we went to Jeremie, where we were to be stationed. Not long after we arrived in Jeremie our contingent commanders advised the Catholics amongst the contingent that we had to go to Thanksgiving Mass for the American Special Forces. I had a very strange feeling about going to this mass, it was like the feeling I had about going to Haiti.

At the mass there were several denominations of nuns present. After the mass, I was immediately drawn to talking to the Sisters of Charities and I found out that they ran a mission that included an orphanage just up the road from the police station where we were working. That interaction with those Sisters was for me the beginning of the support of spiritual friends, a supplication from me asking for more of a relationship with God once again. It wasn't all at once, it took numerous other trips overseas on policing and United Nations missions for me to fully reconnect with God and undo the chains that I had placed upon myself. But I had found faith where I least expected it, in a church in Haiti.

In 2014, I handed in my badge after 31 years with the AFP.... and 35 years of working in government which started as that 17-year-old, joining the Air Force.

For the first little while I just concentrated on keeping running Diversity ACT a community service organisation for LGBTIQA+ people. I just kept working with the people who needed help and doing more in partnering with those who were focussed on similar goals. As a small community organisation there were many financial struggles and I stood for hours cooking sausage sizzles fundraising (which hurts my feet and tendinitis a lot) but with the help of good people we kicked some goals.

We developed a partnership with Tuggeranong Uniting Church which was the establishment of Rainbow Christian Alliance and the Goulburn group, Dare Cafe. The connection with Tuggeranong Uniting certainly ended up taking me on a journey that I never expected.

I also became involved in Kairos Outside for Women which is about supporting women who have been impacted by someone in their lives being in prison. I have also been involved in Emmaus which is about furthering your contemplative journey and leadership.

I found myself undertaking numerous activities with TUC, I became an

Faith stories from women in the pews

elder, found myself on Presbytery Standing Committee, then Presbytery Deputy chair and Presbytery Co-Chair. So many doors opened, one after another, I never expected those doors of leadership and learning to appear as they did and to open so rapidly! I took the opportunities that arose because I want to know more about the running of this organisation called the Uniting Church and my place within it.

Along that pathway of opening doors, I was asked if I had considered a Period of Discernment. After hearing what that meant, my heart sang with joy! Yes, I wanted to undertake those processes and work out with God where I was going, where he wanted me.

Now discernment isn't just an easy black and white decision-making process. Discernment is a journey. Discernment is about what God, and the church wants for me and just not about the things I tell myself.

So, completing my period of discernment, TUC, presbytery, and the candidate selection processes agreed for me to taken on the processes to become a Minister of the Word. I have a lot of work to do, a degree to get through, student placements and of course, I must make it through the other end of the program and still be found suitable.

And personally, I struggle and feel overwhelmed from time to time with the things I have witnessed and lived through as a police officer, but they have shaped who I am.

There is life after policing and for me it is still about serving others and God.

Ever evolving faith

Gwyn's story

I was introduced to the concept of God at church at about the age of four, in a little town in Queensland, there the services were led by a lay preacher who to my young eyes was quite terrifyingly ugly and who spoke with such passion that spittle flew! This was so off-putting that it was a total mystery to me as to why anyone would want to give up a morning to sit in gloom and be tortured. I went to Sunday school which I found uninspiring though I loved the little stickers and the book prizes and the Christmas party, I was in it for the material, not the spiritual.

My father's mother, Granny Elizabeth lived with us up until her death and it was, she, not Sunday School who introduced me to, along with the Royal Family and steamroller mints, the idea of God. She planted a seed of faith and hope within me and gave me a tiny paperback copy of the book of Luke – I can see it in my mind's eye to this day, it had a pretty blue cover and an angelic illustration. I was a voracious reader and I read it many times and slept with it under my pillow.

It wasn't until the age of 14 that any more thoughts of faith or God tapped on my shoulder, I was a typically rambunctious teenager fighting for freedom and fun when a friend asked me to come along to her youth group, so I found myself a part of a Methodist Youth Fellowship or MYF and there more soil was tilled, and more seeds sown. I met my husband Gary at this group, and we became great friends – there's a whole other story there for another time and place!

This was the early '70s and the era of the Jesus Movement and it wasn't until another friend asked me to check out this place of love, acceptance and forgiveness that I finally caught on. I fell into Gods open arms within a month.

Gaz and I did not lose touch and our friendship deepened into love and we married in 1975. I was only 18 and Gary 23 but we had found each other's best friend, we could talk and laugh for hours and still do, it is

Faith stories from women in the pews

this ability to communicate so well, and our shared deep faith in God that has kept us going onward throughout the ordeals of over 24 relocations in 45 years.

Yes, over 24 relocations. I didn't realise what I had signed up for. Gaz was a public servant when we first married, and his position took us to three different towns and six different dwellings before I was 22. It was in Blackall, western Queensland where Gaz responded to the call to the ministry which led us back to south east Queensland and 3 more different homes while he completed his two required degrees.

From there three more moves until we found ourselves in Townsville where life took another turn and Gaz joined the RAAF as a chaplain, by now we had three children and I was becoming increasingly frazzled. We had always laid our decisions before the Lord and had done our best to follow his leading, I have to be honest and admit that I truly detested being a minister's wife. I could never meet the expectations of parishes and quite frankly didn't want to. I had married Gaz and supported him all the way and bore children and was kept busy raising them, I was ever so glad to leave parish ministry.

A chaplain's spouse has a different life altogether, with no expectations upon them and a lot of support available for moves, and there are many moves, many, many moves.

Our first posting was to Canberra and what a blessing it has been, as soon as we found a home to rest our heads, I grabbed the yellow pages to find a place to worship and found Tuggeranong Uniting, and what a find it was. It was the era of the youth group and our two girls were made very welcome, as were we. I can vividly remember that first morning with lots of people and our daughters being swallowed up by the youth group. Wonderful.

The moves kept ticking along and in the first two years of our posting to Canberra we lived in two different houses and were then presented with a quite typical defence dilemma, accept a posting to Malaysia or miss a promotion and possibly gain a poor reputation. We had twelve hours to decide, there was no sleep that night but much, much prayer. Hurray for Jenny and Mary and their families who bravely took on our daughters for the year 2000 as two attractive blonde girls would possibly provide a whole new level of difficulty to our lives both socially and educationally.

We were posted back to Canberra and began our longest stint in one dwelling since Gary's university and college years. We had three years in one place, and it was the most amazing feeling, of course it didn't last, and we were posted to Darwin. I was beginning to feel very worn down, my faith was still strong, but this didn't stop me from beginning to get very stroppy with God. This, coupled with our son Peter's difficulties with constantly changing education systems and the accompanying expectations led us to very carefully consider returning to parish ministry. Miraculously a Canberra parish was in need of a minister and we returned to Canberra to a different life that lasted for three years until Gazza's vocal cords began to give him a lot of grief and he could no longer preach or talk for great lengths of time. Back to the RAAF we went.

Another miracle: we were posted to a position in Canberra and we moved to Jerrabomberra. Gary's boss told him there would be no more postings so, feeling brave, we bought a home… a real home of our own, a giant toy for me, an interior design buff, to decorate, such joy, such answer to years of prayer. We should have known better, before a fortnight in our new home was over, we were posted to Adelaide. I was hanging onto God by my fingernails, grief, anger and depression became my constant companions.

However, God is good, and we were reminded of this very quickly as our home became our eldest daughter's home when she and her family were in dire need of accommodation at a tough time in their lives. Peter moved in with them and his board helped pay their rent and our chickens happily roosted in the coop we provided for them. When I was down, a frequent occurrence, I would remind myself of the Lord's provision for our children, it helped to keep me going.

This was our penultimate posting and from there we were sent to Amberley outside of our hometown of Ipswich. It proved to be a wonderful move where I could reconnect with my siblings and Gaz with his. We lived just five minutes away from Gary's sister who was also my best friend. Many a Friday evening was spent together drinking wine under

Faith stories from women in the pews

the stars and solving the world's problems. From here we were posted back to Canberra and Gaz is now retired, no more postings for us, he works a little part time for the RAAF and is slowly winding it down.

I have become quite adept at walking into new churches and craft groups and joining in, however the constant changes have made me wary of friendship and closeness. I have found myself under the microscope and often judged unfairly once my husband's life calling is discovered. Having a partner who is a minister or chaplain can put a dampener on relaxed conversation and it seems people instantly can feel the urge to clean up their acts and cease to be themselves.

My faith is ever evolving, I believe it is still very strong, but my core beliefs are very different, I started out in my walk with God quite conservative and rule-bound. The constant relocations have shaken me, and I have been forced to constantly re-evaluate where I stand with the Lord and what I believe to be true and important. Perhaps all this upheaval has been instrumental in me being stronger that I ever could have been if we had remained in the one locality, or maybe, just maybe, I'm stubborn!

Faith stories from women in the pews

Sustained by Faith
Enid's story

As a child I was taken to Sunday School by my mother at a very early age and attended weekly with mum and my brother. As I grew older, we often had men from the various church agencies talking about the activities of the mission field including Frontier Services, (then the Australian Inland Mission). I was also involved with the music side of Sunday School and church. I was also part of the Presbyterian Youth Fellowship.

When I left school, after working at a travel agent for 12 months, I went to train as a nurse. I can remember thinking that this was my opportunity to leave behind my church life as I was often working Sunday, or I could make the effort to continue with my spiritual development by reading a chapter of the New Testament every night, to retain that connection. I chose to read the chapter of the New Testament every night and attend church when I could.

After four years I had completed my training and went overseas for eight months. My plan had been to study in America but that did not materialize, so I travelled on my own around America and then Europe. In those days there was no Internet, so I was very aware that the only person who knew where I was, was God!!! Even a letter to my parents took six weeks to get back to Australia, and by then I could have been anywhere. I can remember as I sailed back through the Great Australian Bight, leaning over the side of the boat praying that I was so grateful for my safety that I committed myself to whatever God wanted me to do.

Once back in Australia, I was aware of needing to settle down and remembered the people from Frontier Services that had talked to us during my childhood, so I phoned the office and was told there was a placement in Coen the following April, and this was September. I then did my maternal and child health certificate while I was waiting, then doing specialist nursing and continued attending the church I had grown up in. During this time, I was involved in interesting jobs, such

Faith stories from women in the pews

as Jewish circumcision and other tasks because of my involvement in church activities.

In March I left to go to Coen, and arrived on April 1 with another nurse, both of us twenty-two years of age. We had a hostel of eight school children to look after, cook and take care of the full school term. They were children from the local stations who chose to live with us and attend the local school. Our faith was tested often during this time. We had a Bible reading every morning with the children, which was always interesting as Ann and I had different backgrounds so looked at many readings differently. This was a lesson in itself.

After the two years in Coen, I was married and had two children while living in isolated areas in the Gulf of Carpentaria. As there were no medical facilities, I was again doing the local nursing, and again I relied on my experience and many prayers for guidance in that situation.

When the children needed school, we went back into Cairns but continued to spend a large amount of time on Aboriginal communities, in the Gulf and Cape, again leaning on my faith and experience.

I worked with the district nursing service, for over 20 years and again my faith supported me many times in caring for people particularly in palliative care. I also did my chaplaincy training during this time, hoping to help the other staff with the spiritual side of their assessment tool!!! Always a challenge.

When I "retired," I became Chaplain to the two local hospitals which again tested my faith as I was often the person the staff needed to debrief with and get support as well as the patients. I also worked with many grieving families while helping them with their funerals. After this my journey took me to be the chaplain in an aged cared facility, until I moved to Canberra.

All through my life, I have felt that my faith has sustained me during the tough times and challenges that I have been confronted by, and hope to accomplish in the future.

Surrounded by loving arms

Helen H's story

Eugene and I have been married since 1972. We had retired and had thoroughly enjoyed travelling overseas most years since, with an exhaustive supply of wonderful experiences. On the final night of our last overseas trip our lives were changed dramatically, the date was June 28, 2014.

We spent the night with friends who lived close to Heathrow Airport and were happy to drive us there the following day. During the night Eugene had difficulty navigating the way to the toilet and fell down a steep staircase landing awkwardly fracturing his neck. I reached him minutes later and his words "I can't move my legs."

The next few months were a fog of pain, uncertainty, trying to reach family and friends with the news. It was a nightmare. I was shocked and not thinking clearly.

Doctors delivered news of a life in a wheelchair. I had difficulty absorbing this news.

Surgeons operated to repair the fractured neck and remove the splintered bone fragments. Several days later we were transferred to Shropshire near Oswestry for rehabilitation for three months.

This time was important to enable us to regroup. We had been on a roller coaster, three hospitals, a major operation, no family nearby. We needed time to think, plan to make some sense of our predicament.

I welcomed routine to heal, and my accommodation was nearby and comfortable.

The first Sunday I visited Oswestry Methodist Church and I was surrounded by loving arms and welcomed each week. A couple discovered my love of gardens and drove me most weeks to stately homes in Shropshire and Wales. My camera worked overtime and provided an important diversion.

Faith stories from women in the pews

Nights were long with too many unanswered questions. I sent these to special folk at home and there was always a reply in the morning which was comforting.

I visited Eugene each day; he was struggling with complete bed rest and was losing weight. I think I should explain the procedure. For six weeks Eugene was moved from left side to back and then three hours later to his right side. Three staff were required for this effort. A trained nurse to steady his head plus two staff members either side of the bed. Meals were fed to him and all bodily functions were dealt with when necessary. Eugene had too many hours staring at the ceiling then the wall of his room then a welcome view of the courtyard garden outside.

I left his bedroom late each day and walked the long corridor feeling flat and homesick. We anxiously waited for the end of six weeks of bedrest and after a spinal x-ray we met with the consultant who broke the sobering news. The future would have little progress and Eugene would not walk again. This news hit us hard, and we cried together. The following day we decided we would live life to the full and celebrate each small victory in style. We love each other dearly and we would tackle this challenge together.

After intensive rehab at last we were given the go ahead to fly home to Australia. We were thrilled but very apprehensive. Eugene spent a further four months in the Prince of Wales Hospital, and I shuffled between Sydney and Canberra. This separation was tricky for us both with Eugene in Sydney and me in Canberra, coping with a robbery and trying to modify our home to accommodate Eugene on his return home. After several days I would book a bus to Sydney. It was a welcome time when we both drove home to Canberra. Eugene crouched down in the bus to get a better view of the countryside so missed by us both.

We felt less supported in Canberra with no experts in spinal injury in the A.C.T. but the thought of coming home kept us going but we realized life was very different now.

This is a potted version of our journey since June 28. Eugene's experiences are different from mine. The time since Eugene's fall is peppered with many kind acts of strangers, such warmth and concern, which has powered us on to face another day.

Wonderful friends from Australia wrote regularly and each letter read and reread and cherished. Freddo frogs were distributed among the nursing staff. Australia was talked about until the pain of home became a sharp discomfort that wouldn't go away.

The smallest deeds gave us pleasure, the view of the garden through the window with the change of seasons. Knowing many friends were praying for us helped immensely. We met many warm beautiful people. A very paralysed Pakistani women who sobbed at night and who I tried to comfort. When we left the hospital, we were hugged by her family with comforting words that their god was with us. A retired Methodist minister visited us weekly. We loved his brief visits, and he always left us in a happier frame of mind.

There are downtimes. The inequality of our health system - living life in a wheelchair is fraught with difficulties not encountered until one is living the talk. Footpaths are uneven, culverts vary in steepness, and restaurants are difficult to access. Eating from a table can require a very steady hand. Toilets are rarely wheelchair accessible. Accommodation is not standardised. Respite depends on good friends rather than pay $400 a night for a carer to sleep at home. We have worked hard to give Canberra a Spinal Gym, but there is so much more to be done.

Righteous anger is a valuable driving force but we both know the warm fuzzy feeling of joy and love and being together with those you love.

Faith stories from women in the pews

Called to Care
Norma's story

I was born in 1930 the second child to my mother and father. We lived at North Footscray in a new home building area and some distance from the Footscray township where St Andrew's Presbyterian Church was located. When my father wanted us to start Sunday school there was no bus or other transport available. To get my older sister Doreen there, he rode her on his bike every Sunday afternoon for almost a year. Fortunately, when I was old enough to attend there was a bus service close to our home and I was able to go with my sister. That was the start of my Christian journey.

I remember going at the age of six to a large room in the old part of the church which was the kindergarten and was well set up for the young children. We were gifted with lovely teachers and surprisingly, I remember the song, "Hear the pennies dropping, dropping". The church had built a modern building with a small hall used for the junior children and holding about forty children. There was a second very large building with a stage and wooden pull outs on either side of the hall. We would meet in the centre part of the hall first and then each section would hold a small group of girls on one side and boys on the other side. This is where I believe that the lessons I received from the teachers was the beginning of my journey of faith. We always had lovely music and singing, and I can remember one of my teachers reading Isaiah 53 to us. We had to learn a verse every week and finally I was able to recite the whole chapter. What a remarkable chapter in the old testament. In high school years we had the junior bible study and then the senior bible study. There were groups for boys and girls.

When I was twelve, we were separated, and the girls went into a small hall to Junior Bible Study. The boys had moved into a special part of the new building, a large gymnasium and chapel. At fourteen we went to Senior Bible Study once again in our separate rooms.

At sixteen I was asked to be a Sunday school teacher starting with a group of twelve-year old boys. At that time (1946) we were very short of male teachers. It was a difficult start for me at first, but I thoroughly enjoyed my time with them. After a few years I became the superintendent leading the out-front activities. Later, Sunday School was moved from 3pm to during the 11am Service. As I was in the church choir, I had to forego Sunday School teaching, a journey which I just loved.

I was involved in the Presbyterian Girls Fellowship, which included The Order of the Covenant, every Monday night. We had the choir on Thursday night, Calisthenics on Friday nights and basketball during the winter on Saturday and church three times on Sunday until we changed to two times. Our boys were full time at their gym and had a cricket team. We also wanted to have dancing in our big hall every two months for the now teenagers, but the Church disallowed it. We formed a club called the Ramblers and ran our own dances every two months in the Footscray town hall with the West Footscray Presbyterian teenagers joining us. We also joined them to have day trip competitions in sport. It was on one of these trips that I met my husband Jim who was from the local Methodist Church. Because of all these activities, our 7pm church services were packed with young people, including many newcomers.

Over the years, the girl's fellowship group regularly visited a home for unwed mothers in Fitzroy and we would chat with these young women and take gifts for their babies. I believe it was then I realised what I could do for others in a Christian way.

In 1953 Jim and I married at St Andrew's and after eighteen months purchased a home in Heidelberg West. The home had been built on a block of land owned by the West Heidelberg Church and close to the church. We gave a lot of thought to joining the Methodist Church-simply because it was so close. The church was a small old brick building with a new hall built for a Sunday school and other groups. The sale of our block was the payment for the building.

We were blessed with a very friendly congregation and after the transfer of two ministers over the course of time, we were fortunate to have a Deaconess who arrived from England. She was a truly faithful lady working well with a number of troubled people residing in a poorer area close by. We were active in all areas of the church: Ladies fellowship, Jim in Finance, Seniors' group, Men's society, Sunday school and even tennis at their own court. Our ladies were very involved with caring and during the year we would visit people in the old Kew mental facility which had become home for many unwell people. On some evenings they would have a games night and we were able to join in with the residents.

Our children were baptised here and attended the Sunday School. After fifteen years Jim's firm was transferred to Canberra, and we had to say farewell to our great friends. We arrived in Canberra on Anzac Day. The next week we checked the local paper and found the South Woden Church that met at Pearce School and we joined them the following Sunday. We were only there two weeks when they made an announcement that they needed a parsonage. Jim put his hand up to help as his building firm had just finished building one for a Belconnen Church. The parsonage was built within the year near the Pearce shops.

The church was very well attended and being at the school we were able to have Sunday school in their classrooms. We had to set up weekly in the hall and tidy up afterwards. However, it was well worthwhile, and we enjoyed the fellowship. We had to hold meetings in members' homes as the congregation had been decided earlier not to build a church building, but to put its efforts into the outside world.

One of my friends, a lovely lady was dying of cancer and I visited her regularly. Returning from a visit, I had a dream that night. It was a man's voice telling me that I had healing hands and to use them. Nothing else. This really made me go out and care. My friend died shortly after that visit and I was proud to speak at her funeral. We enjoyed our time at South Woden, Jim with his music, women's fellowship and many other parts of the church life.

In 1991 we really felt we needed to be involved in a church with its own building, as well as full weekly access. We decided to attend Tuggeranong Uniting Church. We were made very welcome and we started attending the 8.30 Service in the chapel. At that time there were three services, very well attended and with lots of young people. We were invited to join a Bible Study group where we met new friends. This group became so big it was divided and we started our Wednesday night meetings which met for many years. We now continue to meet with eight of those members for a monthly social/fellowship lunch.

Soon I realised that the church was just like St Andrews. There were so many things you could do to help with the worship of our God and Saviour. I was involved in reading the Bible in the worship service, choir, flowers, welcoming at the door, morning tea, bible study, teaching children to sew at Fun Sew, fetes and finally the most special one, the Home and Hospital Visitation Team. It was the Visitation Team that I was the most interested in and I realised the answer to my faith calling in caring for others from the dream I had. We were well-mentored by Gwen Miles. Her instructions on how we should operate and care for our congregation when we visited them was excellent. I felt I was able to follow her example with God's help. The years of work with all the members of the team has been amazing. Such faith in action.

For over possibly twenty-five years I believe I have answered God's call. It is surprising how many of our church members were in need of someone to visit, call, or help when in hospital and especially at a time when one of their loved ones was dying. Psalm 23 is one of my favourites and I know it by heart. This is the story of my Christian faith and my call to care.

Faith stories from women in the pews

A grandmother's prayer
Jenny's story

I'd like to share with you a little of my Christian journey, those who have encouraged me along the way and the practices that have kept me on that journey. My journey started with my grandmother who, when she visited from Brisbane, made a point of saying bedtime prayers with me every night.

I see myself as a forever member of my church as I was part of the first worship service that was held in 1975 when the Tuggeranong Valley was opening up. Bill and I married 48 years ago and moved to Canberra, Bill to work in the public service and me teaching in a primary school. We became part of the pioneering folk moving into a new suburb. We were part of the Cooperating Churches of Kambah beginning with 15-20 folk from various denominations. Being involved in a new church brings community and relationship and most of the leadership team were under 30. This led us to become involved in our first small group.

Some 12 months later, the Anglican bishop stepped in, and the Anglicans among us had to worship in another room in the school. We continued with our joint bible study group which later became a prayer and praise group meeting weekly on a Friday night. It was very much like an extended family as few of us had family close by.

But what of my beginning faith experiences. My family did not attend church, but my parents dutifully sent my brothers and me to Sunday school at the local Presbyterian Church. When I was in high school, I joined the youth group and some of the older youth were involved in a group called WEC (Worldwide Evangelical Crusade) with some going overseas to do missionary work. I went along to a WEC meeting with my cousin and very simply made a commitment to follow Jesus. My faith was nurtured by our new minister, the Reverend Ron Sparks who mentored the younger youth group. The youth group became involved in local coffee house ministry. I went to Sydney University studying

Primary teaching and was involved in leading EU Bible Studies there.

Then I met Bill who came to my Church as a theology student to do his practical work. I was the leader of the youth group and I swept him off his feet. We were married later that year and moved to Canberra, with Bill working in the public service and me teaching.

Our prayer and praise group grew as did the babies being produced. It was a very caring group and we looked after each other's children like an extended family. Few of us had family in Canberra coming from Sydney, Brisbane and Melbourne. We grew too big and so divided into two groups and then began our next small group journey for six years. Some of us were elders and church council members. We divided again with new folk joining the church and this is when we met our good friends Cathy and David who came to Canberra from Adelaide. They had a four-year old son, the same age as our son. Our small group was a place of welcome, support, care, study and prayer and praise.

Bill and I have seeded several other small groups while keeping our roots in this group. All these experiences have encouraged me in my faith journey. They have provided nurturing relationships in the presence of Jesus Christ. Life was busy and hectic with three children and a full-time job. But there were desert times, and for me, this was the three years my mother was ill and in a nursing home. Going to Sydney for weekends to support my dad, working full time and managing a family took its toll and my emotional/spiritual bucket became very empty.

I became somewhat depressed, felt alone, and neglected to call on Christ's strength, trying to rely on my own. I ended up withdrawing, avoiding friends and leaving my husband for six months. One of the most vivid memories from those times was our dear small group inviting us both for dessert and coffee and saying how much they loved and cared for both of us and wanted to be there for us. They prayed for us that night. They could have left us to sort ourselves out, but they took a risk, held us and told us they were there for us both.

During those six months we sought counselling and Bill and I both attended an Emmaus walk at Greenhills. With the teaching and special agape love, I handed over to Christ all the relationship anger and frustration and we were gradually able to move on together in our relationship. I learnt to look for the treasure in each other, as focussing on the negatives ends up weighing you down, making me not a nice person to be with. I am very thankful for those special people who prayed for us, loved us and stood by both of us. At that time a special friend Barbara visited me at home, sat with me, listened, and prayed with me.

I guess because I have this wonderful experience of Christian family and my own loving family that I grew up in, I have a passion for facilitating connection and welcoming others. There have been times when my heart would not stop beating quickly because there was a nudge to invite someone home for a meal or into a small group or just call by and see them. As I journey with Christ, I have become very aware of those he is calling me to walk beside. Some days I am much better at doing this than other days and there are times when I am too tired, and work was all too consuming. I found a wonderful work colleague along my journey and we would meet once a week early in the morning before work, walk the streets of Kambah, talk and pray.

Our children grew up and though not church goers, are very loving, caring and supportive of our involvement in the church. I find it easy to love others as I was so loved. Bill is never surprised at who might be at dinner. I have been so blessed by a loving family I cannot help but not pass it on to others. A favourite song from youth days "Pass it on."

> *It only takes a spark to get a fire going*
> *And soon all those around will warm up to its glowing*
> *That's how it is with God's love, once you experience it*
> *You spread his love to everyone, you want to pass it on.*

I encourage you to ask God for opportunities to serve and use your gifts. As we draw closer to God, we are energised to draw closer to others. I have found that keeping that closeness requires regular prayer, reading the bible, worship and spending time with other faithful people.

> *Our love must not be just words or mere talk but active and genuine. This is the proof that we belong to the truth.*
>   1 John 3:18-19

Never be afraid to ask faith questions

Dorothy's story

I was born into a Christian family and at the time I was born my father was the Warden of an Anglican theological college, so I grew up in a scholastic atmosphere based on theology and it was the normal sort of conversation at home. My father was always available, and I felt that you could go into his study and interrupt him at any time. I can remember a blue baize door between the house and his study, but you never felt shut out and could take any little problem to him. It was a great relationship. My father taught me to ask questions and to find out the answers for myself. I did not have to believe anything unless I really believed it.

I think the biggest influence on my faith apart from my family background was the Student Christian Movement at University. It opened me up to other denominations. I had grown up in an Anglican environment and at university I discovered Methodists, Presbyterians, Congregationalists and Roman Catholics, all part of the Christian family. Once at an ACM conference I was asked to give a talk about why I am a Christian. I had never really claimed the title Christian because I felt it was something you worked towards and being a Christian means that you follow Christ and that's a big undertaking. I remember asking my father what on earth I could say. My father said that the Christian life is a search for the truth. You never actually reach it but it grows in richness with progressive achievement. I think this is true. Life is a search for the truth.

I came to Tuggeranong Uniting Church in 1981 when my husband John was appointed as the minister. It was interesting that the same freedom of discussion was consistent with John's upbringing. John came from a Congregational background and the English Congregationalists were good free thinkers and so we fitted very well together. My faith has changed over the years and I have whittled it down to what I really believe. I haven't ever felt forced to believe things just because they are part of the Christian doctrine. I have great difficulty with parts of the

Faith stories from women in the pews

Apostles' Creed and was comforted when a friend behind me in the pews would edit it saying the 'resurrection of the spiritual body' instead of the 'resurrection of the body'. I always felt a great closeness with her.

When I was asked about challenges to my faith the nature of prayer has been a problem because I cannot believe that God or a divine power will intervene in some disastrous situation by responding to prayer. I feel that prayer has a great function in focussing the mind on what you should be able to do in the situation. For example, I believe strongly in the universality of human rights and this has caused me to be involved in Amnesty International over the last 50 years, for 15 years with the Parliamentary Group and, since my retirement, with the local Urgent Action network.

My advice to younger women is to ask as many questions as you need to ask and to work at getting the answers you can accept and believe and live with.

The two verses I have chosen to encourage others are:
John 1:1

> *In the beginning was the word and the word was with God.*

The Greek "logos", translated as Word, for me means truth and when I looked it up in my father's Greek Testament, he had a little notation beside the word saying 'creative realism.'

The other one is 1 John 4:7

> *Beloved, let us love one another for love is of God and everyone that loves knows God, for God is Love.*

That is the basis of my belief. God is Love and this is what we should practise towards everyone. It's a truncated faith but it works for me.

God's guidance and provision
Judy's story

I want to first introduce you to where my journey began, because it is as we grow in faith and years that we can reflect on our journey from our beginning to where we are now and see God's guiding hand as we have journeyed with Him.

I was the first born of three girls born to farmers who lived in fairly remote NSW between Hillston and Griffith. Transport for us and many others was by horse and sulky, which limited a great deal of what we now take for granted- food power, church, social activities, school, medical help to name but a few. We really had a great life, though not always easy. I guess we appreciated each other, enjoyed the beauty of nature and depended on God for farming needs.

My earliest memories of my father are of him tucking us into bed and praying with us each night. "Gentle Jesus meek and mild" was always our beginning prayer. This was good training and a habit and a habit I tried to continue, even during those difficult high school years, even if it was just the Lord's prayer. Train up a child in the way she should go, and when she is old, she will not depart from it. Proverbs 22:6

Church attendance was fairly limited. Combined Protestant, Anglican and Catholic services were held in Merriwagga once a month, and then only if the dirt roads were traversable and a minister available. This did little for spiritual growth and fellowship, but people faithfully gathered and worshipped their Lord.

Scripture at school was an enjoyable time, not frequent but enjoyable and it gave us anther face and another visitor. The twenty students would separate into Protestant and Catholic groups. We really loved Keith. He was with the Bush Missionary Society, an interdenominational mission and placed in Hillston. Keith had one leg, rode a motorbike with a sidecar and played the piano accordion. We sang Wide, wide as the ocean, Build on the Rock, If you're happy and you know it clap your hands... and one could go on and on and there were stories on flannelgraph boards. It was also at this time that Mum and Dad decided to enrol us in correspondence Sunday school in addition to the monthly church Sunday school.

High school years brought changes for me as our nearest school was in Griffith, where my grandparents lived. This brought a change of home, nearness of parents, a large school, a change of friends and several teachers. One of the teachers was Margaret and what a wonderful surprise to find her after 52 years, in this church when we retired to Canberra. It was all quite a challenge for a shy twelve-year old girl, one of God's challenges. I would have been happy to stay at home and do correspondence schooling, but my mother was determined that her daughters would not 'miss out'. Weekends were generally spent at Merriwagga. A train travelled home to Hillston on the Saturday and back to Griffith at 5am on Monday mornings. Weekend life continued much as it always had with friends, dances, movies, tennis, golf, church and family.

On completing the Leaving Certificate, I applied to the Department of Education for a scholarship to study home science, a two-year course only available at Sydney Teachers College and another challenge, one of God's. This was a whole new world and mum had sought accommodation at a small Church of England hostel at Croyden Park. I knew no one, but unkown to me then, a loving God had a plan. Several of the girls worshipped at Croyden Park Church of England and attended youth fellowship there on Sunday evenings so I joined them. It was there that I really grew in my faith and knowledge of Jesus. I learned that I needed to depend more on Him, was loved unconditionally, that He had given His life for me and was there for life's journey. One of the leaders of the fellowship became a good friend and often had some of the hostel girls home for a meal. It so happened that living next door to her was the Secretary of the Bush Missionary Society (remember Keith from Merriwagga school days scripture). The Mission held rallies and information nights in Sydney on the work of the mission in remote areas of NSW and Southern Queensland, taking scripture to schools, church services in remote areas, visiting isolated folk and distributing scriptures. With several fellowshippers going along to rallies, my association and interest in the mission was rekindled.

Towards the end of my first year of college I felt challenged to consider Bible College, but met with opposition from my family. I decided if God wanted my 'services', I could be well used with a teaching certificate wherever that might lead me. The end of 1955 brought job interviews. When asked where I would be happy to go, my response was western area as I had always enjoyed my quiet country childhood. It was quite a large area, and I was surprised to be placed in Bourke, another Bush Missionary Society field area. It was quite a distance from home, as Griffith to Bourke was a 24 hour overnight, three train change journey, and yet another God challenge for me.

The school certainly had its challenge too, having just moved from a central school to an intermediate high school and still all in the one location. We had 12 staff sharing one small room, shared facilities and a new building underway and a flood year. Bourke is surrounded by levy banks to keep the flood waters out but with all the rain that year, there was nearly as much water inside the levy banks as outside the banks. We wore gum boots to school. The whole school community was a caring, friendly and supportive group. Most staff were young and a long way from home. The students were friendly and generally helpful and a number of the teachers quite close in age to the students they were teaching and becoming close friends and I still kept in contact with one of those girls I taught.

It did not take me long to seek out the Bush Missionary Society, become a Sunday school teacher, Girls Brigade leader and do bible study. I was very thankful for God's wonderful provision of that spiritual home. We should never doubt. "Lo, I am always with you" as it is important to leave our concerns and worries with God, leave them there and not take them back and become anxious.

1956 brought Reg to Bourke with the Bush Missionary Society. We shared time in the groups and activities around the mission centre. Reg and I married in December 1959 at my home church in Merriwagga. Reg came from Merrylands in Sydney - God's way of making it a 'merry' occasion- or just coincidence. Together we continued the outreach of

Faith stories from women in the pews

the Mission in the town of Bourke and the Western area with Sunday school, Boys' and Girls' Brigades, adult fellowship, visitation to isolated homes and villages and scripture in the small schools. It was a busy and challenging life and one that I would not have changed.

In 1967 after 9 years and with four small children and the demands that that brings, we decided to move and seek regular employment to give our children opportunities they could not have had in Bourke and to be near my parents. Griffith became our home town. Reg became an electrical fitter and I stayed at home with the children.

During the early years in Griffith, I struggled with depression and at times wondered where my God was. But He has promised to never leave us or forsake us, and I leant very heavily on that promise. Underneath are his everlasting arms and he is there to carry us through. Just trust in him.

We settled very readily into the Methodist church family and Aileen, one of the Canberra folk we met up with again later, was one of those very friendly and caring people who helped us to settle into the church in Griffith. There was a sense of returning home, with family there and some close friends, though many like me had moved away. We soon made more new friends and life returned to its busyness with school children and their activities. Once again, if you are willing, there is always plenty to get involved in around the church no matter where you are.

In 1975 I returned to teaching and I enjoyed the input I had within the school community. Challenges were plentiful in that environment and I did enjoy the sharing and time I had at Wade High School with the opportunities to use my knowledge and skills.

In 1991 and after heart surgery problems it was time for Reg to retire. I moved into casual relief teaching allowing me time to spend with Reg and my elderly mother. This also gave time for both of us to do scripture teaching together in the many small schools around Griffith. The little ones loved Reg's piano accordion playing.

2002 saw us again seeking new directions. With no family left in Griffith, we questioned whether that was where we wanted to be for the rest of our lives. Canberra had always appealed to us, and with family here, it was not a hard decision to make. God's guidance and provision was very evident in this move and we have been very blessed. A favourite hymn is The Great Love of God.

Let me close with a prayer

> *O God, you who are love, the one from whom all love comes*
> *Teach us how to love.*
> *Open our hearts to receive your gift of love.*
> *Shape us into the likeness of Jesus, your Son,*
> *That we may be bringers and gifters*
> *Of love to the world.*
> *Amen.*

Faith stories from women in the pews

I believe in miracles
Julie's story

I am one of the most fortunate people having had a wonderful childhood and raised in a happy Christian home with the most loving of parents, who encouraged and convinced me that I could achieve anything I put my mind to. They built up feelings in me of self-worth and strength that have stuck with me and become tools for survival, giving me the strength to cope with what life was to bring. Their example of a loving relationship with each other and with my brother and me, built the foundation for us children to be the adults and parents we have become.

A relationship is the emotional connection between two people; be it parents, spouse, siblings, children, friends and our God. For that to work it has to be a commitment on both sides that is sincere and genuine, no masks or deception, no abuse or conning with false behaviour. Communication needs to be honest and open with each party sensitive to the other's needs and be ready to listen and forgive.

Relations with others is hard work, but are what life is all about. The valleys and mountain tops we travel are all related to our relationships; the joys, the sorrows, the frustrations, the triumphs. There is nothing more important than the way we relate to people, not only with words but with our actions towards them and our reactions to them.

God is a relational God. His commandment to "Love one another as I have loved you," is clear. We are told to strive to show unconditional love, accepting others as they are, seeing the good in them. This does not mean that we are to be doormats to people who abuse us, and if a relationship is torn down by abuse and violence, addictions such as alcohol, gambling or unfaithfulness in marriage. We must not carry the burden of blame or guilt for the failure of such a relationship. I've learnt we should not take the responsibility for the behaviour of persons who have hurt us in these ways, as they are responsible for their own behaviour and choices.

At age 23, I married a man who gradually deteriorated from a placid, happy-natured social drinker to a binge drinking abusive alcoholic. He became a Jekyll and Hyde. When sober he had no recollection of what he was like when he was drunk, until I'd tell him later. Then he would be remorseful, repentant, gentle and loving, making promises to me with such sincerity that I believed him. He always professed to love me and promised never to hurt me. The promises never amounted to anything.

As the responsibilities of life grew with the arrival of two children, two years apart, he coped by drinking more, often drinking all night and sleeping all day while I looked after the children and the home. He sometimes missed work on a Monday from a binge that began on Friday night, and he would be nasty and abusive until he got over it. Then he would act like nothing had happened.

He was jealous of our two babies taking my time and attention from him, particularly my son, being jealous of male competition. He was detached from having a relationship with them and not involved in their care, even though I desperately needed help, after a caesarean and wound infection both times. I was physically exhausted and in pain for months. It was a huge struggle and only my love for my children kept me going.

In an effort to get him to confront his behavior, I went to a legal aid solicitor to find out my rights should I leave, commencing action to apply for assistance. On his pleas to reconsider and promises to get medical help, I cancelled my application for a legal aid grant. Everything became worse as he combined alcohol with anti-depressants. He became more violent and angry, later described as manic depression. Two years later I was back in the same place, reapplying for legal aid and seeing a counsellor because I sensed his behaviour was leading up to something terrible. One day in his jealousy of our son, then five years old, he strangled our son's pet kitten with his bare hands, as the kitten clawed at his arms, making them bleed. Then lunging at our son with wild eyes and fists clenched, he shouted "And you'll be next!" So, after 11 years of marriage, I left my home in total fear with my five-year old son and three-year old daughter, sheltering in a friend's converted garage.

I was wracked with guilt and regret that I had fought so long and hard to save this relationship, thinking I could fix everything because marriage was meant to be forever. Should I have handled things differently? Perhaps been more aggressive? Less patient? Less resilient? I know God created me as a passive person; a peacemaker. I knew I was strong, but I believe I tried too hard and for too long until we were all in danger.

After our separation he kept drinking while on medication, even though he said he wasn't, becoming more disturbed and more violent. Because he had not built a relationship with his children and was so detached from them, they didn't even realise he wasn't with us anymore. How sad was that! I thought he was becoming almost suicidal, not coping on his own, but he was too much of a coward to turn his violence on himself and decided after a few months alone that I was the reason he was hurting and so he decided to hurt me to make it fair, in fact, to kill me.

He drove to my recently allocated Government house at 7pm on 6th October 1989, apparently after a drinking binge of several days and launched himself through my lounge room window with an axe, stabbing me with a jagged hunting knife in front of my three-year old daughter. My son was in Sydney at the time staying with my parents. He slashed my wrist and drove the knife through my right hand each time I tried to raise my hand to pick up the phone or get to the door to escape. Chasing me to the house opposite, he caught up with me at their front door, pinned me against the wall and stabbed me several times in the neck and through the mouth.

At one stage he drove the knife through the jawbone. I could see blood pumping from my neck and spraying the brick wall on their porch, pooling on the ground. My clothes were soaked in blood. With my knowledge of anatomy, as an operating theatre nurse and the amount of blood loss, I believed I would soon die. I prayed to God to please keep my little daughter safe.

You can imagine the shock for those people who opened their front door to see me in that state. As someone tried to pull me in the door, my attacker was pulling my head back by my hair and I could see his arm swiping with the knife at my neck for what seemed an eternity. Several people from the house got behind him to pull him off. Eventually his grip broke and he ran to his car and drove away, to be apprehended by police. I was six hours in surgery that night and three weeks in hospital.

I believe in miracles. You can't deny miracles happen when you have been on the receiving end, and blessed by them. There were many miracles that night, that showed me not only was God real, but he was right there and had sent people to be his angels to help me.

Survival was a miracle and through all this I remained alert and didn't even lose consciousness. This defied explanation. My daughter was unharmed. She was calm and strong, unfazed by the scene and the sight of me, helping the ambulance men to attend to me and giving the most grown-up words of encouragement and comfort to me that only God could have given her - a three-year old. This whole experience really impacted on our already close relationship, as she has always believed that if she hadn't helped that night to press the towels on my wounds I would have died. She is very caring and protective of me still. That my son not being there probably saved his life too, as his father, in his jealousy and rage, I believe, would have surely stabbed him as well.

A man I had met twice recently at a sole parent support group had been passing by on his evening shift meal break and decided to call in for a cup of tea. He arrived only a few minutes before the attack. He sustained several minor stab wounds, risking his life to help me; someone he barely knew. Without him I would never have been able to break free and run to the house across the road. The neighbours at the house I ran to, whom I had never met, happened to be at home with visitors and were beautiful Christian people who were not afraid to help.

Throughout my time in hospital and trips to the surgery I was carried in the arms of my family and friends, surrounded by love and prayer; God's people bringing His love and healing to me. I was so overwhelmed by all this love and support, so overawed and relieved that I had even survived, that I remained cheerful and strong with a calm peacefulness that amazed everyone. I am sure that only through the prayers of many did I receive healing far beyond medical expectations. My family in Sydney and Adelaide organised prayer chains. Initially my face had some

Faith stories from women in the pews

paralysis on one side and was a little crooked as if I'd had a mild stroke. After a week I woke up one morning and it was restored, as it is now. My father who had come down from Sydney, visiting me every day, proclaimed this to be miraculous. The surgeon was stunned.

After five operations, a great deal of reconstructive plastic and micro-surgery and years of dental work I am left with nerve and muscle damage to my face, mouth and right hand and compromised nerve supply to my right vocal cord, making speaking and singing very difficult. Miraculously the nerve supply to my left vocal cord was intact, other-wise I would have had no voice at all.

I had a lump on my chest where the point of the knife had penetrated just above the heart area. I thought, "Thank you Lord! That was pretty close." I will never forget hearing the ambulance officers saying that my right carotid artery, was visible. I knew another millimeter or two and I'd have been history, instantly. When the staff in hospital were eventually able to get past the drains and dressings on my neck to wash my hair a week later, a large amount of hair at the back fell out, held there only by dried blood. The hair had been pulled with such force it had literally been pulled out by the roots!

My right hand hadn't much resembled a hand that night and in my despair I thought I may never be able to use it again. However, after a few months I was back at work assisting in the operating theatre, although with much difficulty, learning to be left handed as much as possible. Yet more answers to prayer. I had to work to survive and persisted with physiotherapy for two years. For several years after the attack, I experienced random sharp pains in my face, with muscle spasms that would contort my face and mouth. This made me feel self-conscious thinking that people could see it happening. For 13 years after the attack I still had that 'after dentist' feeling of numbness and swelling that people complain about; the feeling which only takes a few hours to wear off. The blessing of "Healing Hands" over the years has resulted in partial return of feeling in my face.

After my husband was locked up that night, I never saw him again, except from a distance at a committal hearing. He has never contacted me or spoken to me. He spoke out in the newspaper to say I was a wonderful wife, he'd always loved me and I'd done nothing to deserve what he did to me. He admitted that it was the effects of alcohol, and he deserved to be punished for what he had done. I've always wished he could have just written and said sorry to me. It would have made forgiveness easier.

He went to prison, his working career over and we were on our own, no maintenance, no child support and no contact. We had lost our lovely family home, a home I had loved and nurtured. This event had brought a final closing to our relationship. I believe God had released me from this marriage. I could finally divorce him. No one ever contacted me to inform me of his progress with alcoholism, his state of mind, his intentions regarding me and the children, or his whereabouts after release. I only learnt of him being paroled two and a half years after the attack through a casual conversation with his mother. For years I felt afraid, feeling I could never trust him again and looking over my shoulder everywhere I went.

I can well imagine how difficult and challenging it would be maintaining a relationship with a family member in prison, trying to manage to keep the home running as smoothly as possible whilst standing by the person in prison. Even though that didn't apply to us, it all still impacted hugely on our family, financially and emotionally. Allowing my children to maintain their close relationship with my attacker's mother, their Nana, had its stresses and strains.

My son at five was devastated just knowing he had a father who could do such a thing to his mother and who had not wanted him from the start. Instead of a father to have a relationship with, like many of his friends, his father was in jail.

My son had no self-confidence and my heart ached for him. He became over-protective of me, feeling guilty that he hadn't been there on the night of the attack, believing that maybe he could have helped in some way. At age six he took a karate course to help protect me and his little sister, his idea. As I have reassured him and built him up over the years, we've maintained a very strong and loving relationship.

Faith stories from women in the pews

My daughter has maintained the strength she showed that night, her attitude from the age of three was always "we've all survived - God saved us - my rotten Dad's gone now and good riddance!" She never had nightmares, she never bottled things up and would just blurt out her memories and feelings spontaneously, anywhere, anytime. I think she is a miracle, as she's never been bound by bitterness, anger or fear. She's strong and beautiful and loves God and life. Ruth was a special person who was most instrumental in these healing prayers and the encouragement I needed to persevere. What an awesome joy and privileged relationship. We really need to nurture and treasure our special friendships.

I hardly played music during my marriage, I didn't have the time or will and I didn't feel good enough. I had no contact with other musicians. After the attack physically I couldn't play music. I would have painful muscle spasms that would contort and lock my hand like a claw. I also had numbness and reduced movement in my fingers. Some years later, prayer ministry with some dear friends in my church led to these spasms stopping in my hand and face and I was able to become active in music ministry. I look at what God has done directly and through other people for me and my relationship with Him has grown.

Eighteen months after the attack, Keith, the man passing by who helped me that night, and every day after, married me. God had surely sent him to us. My children and I were loved and treasured and cared for as we had never been. We were all so happy for a short time. He later became ill with cancer and following a terrible six months in hospital died shortly after our third wedding anniversary. To make sense of this I had to focus on the happy memories and positives. With him we experienced the best of relationships, a wonderful husband, loving father and a great role model for the children, building them up and loving them as his own. What a blessing! I cannot imagine how life would have been for me in those few years following the attack without him. He was a godsend, a beautiful man.

Those six months he was in hospital was very painful. Keith knew he was dying. Sadly he couldn't face that with me. Without realizing it shut us out when we desperately needed him. He firmly believed that he would get better. In an effort to love and protect us he denied us the right to deal with this together. Keith and I needed to share our fears in order to prepare ourselves. We needed to say important things to each other, before it was too late. He told the nurses that the little time he had with me had made his whole life worthwhile, but that he couldn't say goodbye to me. While he thought he was sparing me from more pain, in fact in his loving kindness he did not fully realize what I needed most. In my grief I wondered where God had gone, having brought Keith to us in our time of need and then taken him away. We were devastated once more. My children were only seven and nine.

Yet again, God sent his people to help me. Not just family, friends and workmates, but also my new church family I had joined the year before. These people showed me by their actions what being a true Christian means. They blessed us through their friendship, prayer support, phone calls, visits, meals, flowers and food hampers. They gave help with everything from home maintenance to childcare and transport, even financial assistance. It brought us so much comfort when these kind people showed unconditional love to me and my little family with simply a hug, a hand to hold, an arm around shoulders, patient ears to listen and kind words to reassure. They brought joy and laughter when we were sad.

On the day of Keith's funeral his workmates gave me a cheque for a large amount of money they had collected between them. It paid for the funeral with an amount left over. Returning to work a week later my work mates presented me with a collection of money and personal cheques from the doctors and nurses. My boss made it possible for the children and I to go on a holiday, giving us time to just love and comfort one another. Shortly after our return a special friend organised a surprise fortieth birthday party for me. This made me feel wonderful, filling our sad home with fun and laughter.

Needing to downgrade to a smaller mortgage, my church family organised some working bees to prepare my house for sale. Because of all these people and their Christian ministry to me I was reassured that God was always there. I never lost my faith, my hope in the future or my sense of humour.

Some years later I had the privilege of attending the Kairos Outside weekend in Sydney as a guest and it was exactly what I needed. I realised that I was carrying things in my heart that I needed to confront and release, to lay to rest forever, to be a whole and free person. I didn't want to carry the load that weighed me down any more and I no longer wanted brick walls left standing in my life built from fear, anger, bitterness, hurt and un-forgiveness; walls which could block relationships from wholeness, with God or with people. I realised that while one can't forget, we must forgive, and I prayed for help to do that. As the weekend unfolded, I found for the first time a will to forgive my first husband and to wish him well. I recognised the need to forgive Keith for dying and leaving me, and not saying goodbye. Restoration is a word that is on my mind constantly. Restoration: achievable, essential, powerful. The weekend had been a turning point; God gave me the will, desire, courage and strength to lay all these things to rest and accept healing in my spirit.

Over the years that followed I have kept my belief that God was looking after me. I chose to strive to always celebrate my life and survival. I chose to keep the joy in my heart and my love of people always. I have constantly found that God has put people in my path along the way, when I have needed them the most.

Despite difficulties with my physical injuries, to my hand, mouth and voice, I continued to persevere in my nursing career, which I loved so much. I eventually retired after 47 years of nursing; including the last 41 years in the Operating Theatres. I was blessed with the very humbling privilege of assisting the surgeons who operated on me after the knife attack.

I grew in strength and confidence, gained promotion in my career, taught and guided staff, and continued to gain the respect of surgeons in all surgical specialties. With the additional healing the Lord has granted me in my right hand, I was able to assist in all surgeries, everything from Orthopaedic joint replacements to the most intricate and delicate micro surgeries. My driving force to help people, my patients, their families and my wonderful colleagues was fulfilled in the ministry of my nursing. If I had my life over again, I would not choose another career.

In 2003 I was blessed to meet Michael, a beautiful Christian man who was teaching at Erindale College, right near my church family at Tuggeranong Uniting Church. I soon discovered he worked with people I knew, and was teaching the offspring of many families I knew through the Church. It became obvious that he was a very caring, kind and compassionate man, a wonderful teacher with a strong faith in God, love of life, and many shared interests.

He brought great joy, encouragement, love and support to my life. He built me up in helping me to continue to heal from all the tragedy and sadness in my life, and to become stronger and more self-confident. When we married, our wedding song was "You Raise Me Up" – (to more than I can be); a beautiful recording by Celtic Woman.

In the year 2000 I became active in the Canberra Monaro Folk Society, regularly playing my 12-String guitar. I have run a large group within the Society since 2005. Every week we play music at various venues, including at members' homes, the Canberra Irish Club, The Irish Embassy, community events and concerts, retirement communities, dances and private events. We have a very large membership, and repertoire. This brings great joy and wonderful friendships, while growing our skills and using the gifts God has given us.

In 2010, finding myself unable to play my guitar due to a frozen left shoulder, Michael encouraged me to try a smaller instrument. This enabled me to keep playing the music I love so much. Realizing I was in love with the Celtic mandolin, I began a journey of determination and perseverance, teaching myself this beautiful instrument. Now in 2021, I am quite overwhelmed and excited at the success of this challenging endeavour and of the doors it has opened. Besides playing in the Folk Society, I have played mandolin on cruise ships as a much-welcomed guest with the professional musicians … on seven cruises now - an absolute dream come true!

For the past five years, I have been playing with the Canberra Mandolin Orchestra, with the First Mandolins; string heaven! I have been privileged to be part of two CDs with the orchestra, and have performed with them at many wonderful venues in Canberra and surrounds.

While we all face our fears and insecurities I know there is no limit to God's love and healing power. We can overcome all that is placed in our path. Don't focus on endings, only on new beginnings. God carries us through dark valleys and walks with us on the mountain tops. It is my prayer that God keeps his hand on your shoulders and blesses all your new beginnings. I pray that my story brings hope to your life and inspires your faith. We must never underestimate the power of prayer, when others intercede and pray for us. So pray for each other whenever you can.

Despite the challenges I have faced, I have never lost my faith in God's plan for me. My heart has ached for my children with the traumas they too have suffered, and I continue to pray for them both in their struggles. I believe in miracles. They can and do happen. Praise God!

This Bible verse speaks to me:

> *For surely I know the plans I have for you, says the Lord, plans for your welfare and not for harm, to give you a future with hope.*
> Jeremiah 29:11

A life lived on three continents
Pam's story

The beginning and ending stages of my life were, and are, pretty ordinary, but looking back over the span of years in between, I feel so privileged to have had travels and sights and experiences which as a youngster I could never have imagined. We go through different stages in our lives that cause us to adapt to different experiences.

I was born in 1930. My childhood was in England, living in various places in the Home Counties, Hertfordshire and Essex mostly, and ending up in a little village in a small cottage, two up and two down. The front door opened directly into the front room, there was a tiny scullery at the back with a cold-water tap, no bathroom, and an outside toilet. My primary school was a two-roomed, two teacher school with an asphalt playground, but surrounded by fields, and to which I walked about two miles. This was followed by a good education in a grammar school in the town of Bishop's Stortford, which was reached by a three-mile bike ride, then a train ride. I loved school and did well academically, and also loved sport. This was during the war-years, I was nine when the Second World War broke out. Living not far from London we experienced some trouble with nearby air raids, but nothing serious. My father volunteered for the army at the beginning of the war and served the war out in Europe.

At the end of the war my parents divorced, one of the many marriages that could not survive the terrible experiences so many serving soldiers had gone through. My father suffered post-traumatic stress disorder, mostly, I believe, caused by his experience going with his men to liberate the Nazi concentration camp of Belsen, and the terrible things he saw there. We became a female only household, consisting of my mother, my grandmother, who came to live with us after Grandpa died, and my older sister, Jill. She was a rebellious teenager. I think she had been very close to our father. She left school without taking the exams and in 1949, as soon as she turned twenty-one, left the boring village and the austerity of post-war England and migrated to Canada. At that time, I had no idea that I also would leave England.

I was the first one in my family to take up tertiary education. The traditionally accepted role for girls like me was to find 'Mister Right' and settle down to marriage, children and home life, while husbands were expected to go to work and provide, and I never envisaged anything different. However, I was good academically, so my headmistress encouraged me to aspire to a university education, and arranged a grant for me. My mother was happy with this as she felt teaching qualifications would protect me from the poverty she experienced when she was left with no support and no qualifications for a job after the war. I got a place in Bristol University, got a degree and trained as a teacher. I studied French, merely because it was my best subject at school, and that was nice because during our first year we had to live for six months in Paris. However, as it happened, I didn't teach for long afterwards, as I had met my future husband, Jim Pelling, at university, and in 1954 got married and accompanied him overseas.

Jim was from Brighton in Sussex, had studied at Theological College in Bristol and afterwards applied to work for the London Missionary Society. We were both members of the Congregational Church. He was accepted and appointed to work in Southern Rhodesia (now Zimbabwe). He was ordained, we got married, and three weeks later we boarded a ship of the Union Castle Line and sailed away. Two weeks later, in May 1954, we were in Africa, arriving at Cape Town, where we boarded a train and journeyed north for three days, and – lo and behold- we were in Rhodesia! I was 24 years old. I had never dreamed I would go to Africa, let alone live there! We stayed there for 39 years and loved it, never wanting to go back to England to live.

Africa had been colonised by European countries and Christian churches from all denominations had been established there. It was in Southern Rhodesia where the London Missionary Society had sent missionaries to spread Christianity and eventually establish Christian communities, churches, educational and medical work. We were sent first to a small mission station in Lupane where there was a primary school, consisting of several cement-block classrooms, a small mud-walled church building, a house for us to live in, and no missionary colleagues. There was no electricity, no telephone, water pumped up from a bore-hole by hand, and a little black wood-burning stove for cooking. A strip road led to the country's second city, Bulawayo, about three hundred kilometres away, where we usually went once a month for supplies, driving in a little small-wheel-based Land Rover. There was a Roman Catholic mission hospital about halfway which could be visited in emergency.

We had about eighteen years living on several different mission stations in the bush, but often had missionary colleagues, mostly teachers, with a small clinic run by a missionary nurse. We learned about the people's culture and their traditions, including their music and singing, which was of great interest to me. Jim learned the local Ndebele language very well. Our three children were born during these years; I used to go and stay with friends in Bulawayo for two weeks before the estimated time of birth and have the babies in the maternity hospital. Sounds simple, doesn't it? But here's a little story.

Expecting my first baby, with no family around, I knew practically nothing about pregnancy, birthing and babies, and there were no antenatal classes for me to attend. However, my nice GP in town, who gave me check-ups once a month, provided me with a little booklet which explained it all. So we calculated the dates and planned to travel into town in plenty of time before the birth. A few kilometres from our mission, on the road to Bulawayo, there was a river spanned by a low-level bridge. It was January, in the middle of the rainy season, and that year the rains were unusually heavy, and the river came down full and fast, flowing over the bridge, preventing vehicles from crossing. We waited unfazed for the water to go down, for, after all, our baby wasn't due for at least another couple of weeks, was it?

When we arrived at the mission station near Bulawayo where I was to stay with friends and colleagues, we discovered that Ken and Mavis, colleagues from yet another mission station in the bush, were there too, as Mavis was expecting her first baby at the same time as me. Jim and Ken went back home. Two days later Mavis and I had our babies on the same night, Ken was telephoned the news and straightway drove back to the hospital to see his wife and new baby girl. As Jim could not be reached by telephone, Ken sent off a telegram to him to announce the news of my delivery of a baby boy. It went via the government village nearby where lived the administrators of that tribal area. An African messenger cycled to our mission to hand Jim the telegram form which read: "Son born this morning both well Ken." Jim read the message and said to himself: "That's nice, Ken has a son" and went on with what he was doing. Well, our baby wasn't yet due, was it? No need to spell out for you how he was received when he finally got the message and arrived to see his wife and new son two days later!

My husband's job was to serve as minister to the Christian congregations already established by others, and to travel around the district to visit the primary schools established there by the missions, checking on the teachers, paying their salaries, and transporting school supplies to them. He learned to speak the local language well, the Ndebele Language, spoken around the Bulawayo area, and preached in it. He would camp out at the bush schools, usually for a week at a time, while I stayed home alone to look after the children.

I got involved with the African women, mostly through being expected to take part in their Women's Association, like a Mothers Union. To me, as a young woman out from England, who had never been to such a meeting in my life, it was all very strange. All the different church denominations had their women's associations, which met once a week, and they had a uniform: a black skirt with a coloured blouse, different colours for the different denominations: Methodist – red; Anglican – blue; LMS – yellow.

As the minister's wife I was expected to wear the uniform on Thursday afternoons and attend the meetings for a little service, with hymn singing and a little preaching or Bible study, sometimes some handwork or a cooking recipe. No men were allowed, and it was only married women who could be full members of the association. When new women came to join, I had to perform the little ceremony of accepting them, when they were allowed, with great pride, to put on the uniform. I learned how to take part and sometimes went to camp with them when they had conferences somewhere in the area. I got to know some lovely people who became my friends.

Faith stories from women in the pews

My Christian background hadn't really prepared me for the life of a missionary's wife. My mother and father were not church goers when I was a child, but I was sent to a Sunday school run by an elderly Methodist lady, learnt basic Christian teachings and sat the Sunday School Exams. As a teenager I joined a youth group run by the minister of the little Congregational chapel in a nearby village and enjoyed singing hymns and Christmas carols in the services. As a student in Bristol, I still loved singing so joined the University Choral Society, while I continued to attend Sunday services at a Congregational church in the town. I also joined a student Congregational Society meeting run by students studying at the local Theological College, which is where I met Jim. I thought it would be a fine thing that in marrying a missionary I could be doing work for the spreading of Christianity, though I had never met a missionary working in a foreign land, knew nothing about what it would entail, didn't know where Rhodesia was in Africa, nor anything about its history. Well, at least I was used to Sunday services and hymn singing!

African worship services had plenty of singing, done unaccompanied in four parts. The hymn book used had the music printed in tonic sol fa, with the words, most hymns being known Protestant hymns translated by the first missionaries into the local language. I taught myself to read the notes in tonic sol fa and enjoyed singing the alto part to many familiar tunes.

After nearly twenty years living in the bush, the next years of our life were spent in the city. In 1973 we moved into the city of Bulawayo, where Jim continued to work in the African churches in the townships. I too, learned to drive around the narrow alleyways to go to the women's meetings. We rented a house in a white suburb and so had all mod-cons and we were near shops. Social life for me and the teenage children opened up and we made new friends. I bought a second hand piano and found a lovely choir to join which was run with African singers from a teacher training college for African students.

A little bit more about my husband's work: Since he was a good student of the local language of the people in the southern part of Rhodesia, Ndebele, he was asked to do some translation work for the Church. The Ndebele people were using a Zulu Bible produced in South Africa.

Faith stories from women in the pews

Zulu was the language out of which Ndebele had originally come, so it was near enough for people to understand at first, but a hundred years later the languages had moved further apart and the translation needed revising. Jim was asked to undertake this task, together with an Ndebele colleague, Reverend. Mzilethi, while continuing their normal church work. There was a lot of committee work with representatives of the different denominations, which involved a great deal of typing, correcting and re-typing, before the age of computers. They ended up making a completely new translation, published in 1976, printed locally, and still used there by Christians of many denominations.

During our lives in Africa, we lived through times of great turmoil and change, so I think my story needs to touch on some of that history. The Rhodesia we arrived in had a white government and was very colonial, privileging the whites and oppressing blacks. The Africans were second class citizens, they were pushed off the best land and practised mostly subsistence farming in crowded tribal trust lands, and kept the few cattle the government laws allowed them. Traditionally they were farmers, and the land issue was the greatest cause of grievance, both then and now, and a main cause of the struggle for independence from white minority rule. (My quotes in this section come from a book "The Struggle for Zimbabwe" by David Martin and Phyllis Johnson, published in 1981.) "In 1961 more than one third of the land was held by Europeans, who numbered only one-seventeenth of the population. Almost all the best land was in the hands of 7,800 white farmers; the Tribal Trust areas, less fertile land, carried fourteen times the population."

Another major frustration and a real grievance for the people was lack of educational opportunities. Education for African children was minimal, a survey in 1972 showed that "Less than one-third of Africans aged eighteen and nineteen had formal education beyond the third year of primary school. Less than 6% of Africans in this age group were fortunate enough to get secondary school places and only two African children in every 1,000 reached the sixth form (Years 11 & 12)." On the other hand, the white people's children, including ours, had excellent schools to go to. I taught my children myself using the government Correspondence School for the first two years. After that, when we still lived in the bush, there was boarding school for the boys in Bulawayo, and they came home for holidays.

There was discrimination in everything in those times. Segregation was in force in the towns in housing, education, jobs and socially. There was discrimination in wages, there was discrimination in medical care. Medical care for white people was of a high standard, there was minimal care for Africans. Most of the medical care in the rural districts was provided by the missions, but "It was estimated in 1971 that there was only one doctor for every 45,556 people in the rural areas," and of course the land was not densely settled, the people were scattered over distances. The situation became much worse during the following years when 50% of the missionary doctors had to flee from the dangerous areas into the cities.

This, of course, brings me to the troubled time of guerrilla insurgency, when the African 'freedom fighters', ('terrorists' to the white government) were fighting for their right to reclaim their country, be full citizens and achieve independence from minority white rule. The War of Independence intensified during the nineteen-seventies. It was similar to any other guerrilla war, a time of hardship and suffering to many people in certain areas of the country, a time of brutality and death on both sides. I and the family were already away from the dangerous areas in the bush, living in town throughout the seventies when the trouble intensified. Other white missionaries, teachers, nurses, moved into town. Some stayed in the bush, some were killed. I could tell you lots of stories about that time, of what happened to black friends and white friends. It was a time when the 'winds of change' were blowing over the African colonies. Kenya, Malawi, Tanzania, Zambia, Botswana had already become independent. All Ian Smith, our Prime Minister, could say was "not in my lifetime": he was wrong. Independence came in 1980, and independence leader Robert Mugabe easily won the first election in which the African population had voted.

In 1979 we had moved again, to settle in the capital city, Salisbury, now called Harare, where Jim started a new phase of his career, teaching theological students at the Theological College, and I went back to school teaching, getting a job to teach French in a government second-

Faith stories from women in the pews

ary school for boys, a new life for me too. Two of the children, Simon and Karina, went away to university in Cape Town, while the eldest, Andrew, married and went to work in Botswana, having completed a compulsory term of National Service during the Independence War. All three eventually migrated to Australia and have made good lives here with their children.

It was an exciting time to live through in the new Zimbabwe, a time of great change. There have, as everyone knows, been hard times for the country and the people through the years since then, but I want to tell you a little about the good things that happened after independence. Segregation ended, the colour of your skin was no longer a bar to anything, housing, jobs, education, medical help, or participation in government. This was all made possible by a huge explosion of services in the world of education. Great strides were made in the expansion of education, especially secondary education, and so the black middle class grew. The school where I was teaching was transformed, black students were bused in from a nearby black township, and black teachers were teaching alongside white teachers. Accelerated teacher training programmes released more and more teachers to do the job.

Huge strides were made in the area of health also, training of doctors and nurses, opening up the big hospitals to all patients, building and staffing of more clinics in the rural areas, and so on. Government ministries and departments and municipal offices were staffed more and more by Africans; many more black lawyers trained and practised. Robert Mugabe was a clever, highly educated man and lauded everywhere in the eighties as an admired independence leader. What developed in later years, with much hardship and suffering, is another story, and not the purpose of this little autobiographical account to recount.

Thirty-nine years of my life were lived in Zimbabwe, and – yes, the bush country, Victoria Falls, the game parks and the wild animals were a part of it all, and the brave, but basically gentle people, whom I remember with great fondness. We left there in 1993, the year of Jim's retirement, and were fortunate to be accepted for residence in this lovely country of Australia, where our three children had come to settle in the eighties. Now, with Jim gone- he died in 1999- I have another life in old age, living on my own in a nice retirement village, with children, grandchildren and great-grandchildren both near and far.

I am writing my story in the year 2018. In this last stage of my life, for nearly twenty-five years, I have been blessed to have been able to be involved with my wonderful friends in Tuggeranong Uniting Church in Canberra. I have always felt that as a Christian one has to contribute to the welfare of others in some way without receiving monetary payment. I did also accept the fact that for ministers' wives, especially 'back in the day,' this was a given. Except for the ten years when I received a government salary as a teacher, I have always found voluntary work to do and enjoyed it. (But I remember clearly the day I received my first pay cheque, I couldn't quite believe it – I was actually being paid money for the work I had done! It was a great feeling.) At TUC I have enjoyed making some contribution to the life of the church, teaching a Sunday School class or helping a youth group occasionally, in the days when there were larger numbers of children and young people in our church. For many years I led a bible study group for some members of the congregation interested in 'progressive Christianity'. That particular activity meant a lot to me, I changed my ideas and grew as a Christian in a freeing kind of way, and I hope it helped the faithful friends as we shared ideas within the group and studied some new books or videos.

My other source of pleasure and a little pride during these years has been my role in the provision of music for the congregation. Up until a few years ago, I have played either piano or clavinova for services, leading and accompanying congregational singing, usually with my good friend Jim playing his saxophone. I no longer have a voice for singing, but I have enjoyed leading singing groups and finding new church music – we have had a lot of fun together. On the odd occasions when the preacher chooses to ask the congregation to sing an African song found in the Together in Song hymn book, my mind flies back to the times I heard African voices singing, unaccompanied, in four voice harmony. The way the song is presented in our church service is always disappointing to me, but the memories are there of another time, another place, other people.

I am now an old woman content with a quiet life and grateful for good times spent with friends. As it is in everyone's life, I have experienced hard times as well as good times. There have been illness and worry, loneliness and boredom, resentment and helplessness, but I have always called on God to take my burdens and see me through, and that is what has happened. Thankful for God's continuing care, I consider myself blessed to have had a life of great opportunities and varied experiences.

Faith calls for action

Cathy's story

Looking back, I realise that I was incredibly fortunate in my family background and upbringing. My mother was a scientist who came from an Irish/Australian Presbyterian family with a strong support for female education and for social justice, and my father was an atheist (probably a result of his years as a fighter pilot during the war) but he had the highest ethical standards of anyone I ever knew.

Mum made sure that we went to Sunday School when we were young, and when I was a teenager, I started going to the youth group at the local Anglican Church with my friends. I could really identify with the Jesus who cared about the poor and the disadvantaged, and who was never frightened of standing up to injustice or cruelty.

I became a follower of Jesus in my mid-teens, though it is probably fair to say that I have lived with doubts ever since then about the nature of God over the millennia and across the universe.

After I finished university, I headed off overseas. My father was very keen for all of us to get an education and then see something of the world before 'settling down', but I don't think even he expected me to travel overland from Kathmandu to London, to meet the love of my life on that journey, to get married in the UK and to be away from Australia for over 2 years.

Meeting and marrying David was the best thing that ever happened to me. The guys I had previously gone out with were nice, caring but fairly conservative fellows, and I had always had a hankering for someone who would match me in an interest in the world, a desire to make the world a better place and who would love me as I was (not especially attractive and filled with self-doubt).

When we returned to Australia in 1976, we settled in Adelaide, found jobs and bought a house there. We attended an Anglican church. It was more conservative than we would have liked, but the warm welcome and the friends we made there encouraged us to stay. Michael and Melanie were both born in Adelaide, but it was when Melanie was a baby that the firm of consulting engineers where Dave was working closed their Adelaide office and offered him a job in Canberra.

We had not really considered Canberra before, but its closeness to my family in Sydney was a big attraction. We came to Canberra towards the end of 1982, to a rented house in Torrens. Some friends in Adelaide, who had come from Canberra, suggested that we might like to try the Uniting Church congregation that was establishing itself in Tuggeranong, known at the time as 'nappy valley'.

Our first experience of the TUC congregation was in the Urambi Primary School hall, where they were meeting at the time. Over morning tea, I asked, in some desperation, if anyone had a boy around age four. Jenny said that she did and promptly invited me for lunch the following week. Over a chatty lunch, while the boys played outside, we even discovered that our mothers played golf at the same golf club in Sydney!

A couple of months later, I realised that I was pregnant again (and being horribly unwell for three months). Jenny and the other members of the small group, which by then we had joined, were incredibly supportive. We were all young families and mostly without family support in Canberra, so our church community and small groups in particular provided very important support networks.

As the TUC community expanded, the inconvenience of meeting in school halls became a catalyst to a serious fund-raising effort towards building our own parish centre. When the chair of the building committee had to step down for health reasons, I was asked to take on the task. The committee members were a fantastic group to work with and I well remember going to meetings with architects and builders with a toddler in tow (though fortunately James was a very easy-going child). More than anything, the role gave me much-needed confidence, and practice in public speaking. In 1988, the vision became a reality when the new centre was officially opened.

My ongoing desire to solve some of the world's problems changed focus in 1989, when I was asked to be a candidate for the ACT's first self-government election on the community-based Residents Rally ticket. I wasn't elected, though four of our group were, and the whole experience gave me an appreciation for the political process and the importance for people who care about outcomes to get involved.

In more recent years, now that we are retired from the paid workforce, Dave and I have become climate and environmental activists. The science is so clear, that the world is heading for a catastrophe if emissions are not drastically cut in the next few years, and, of course, the people who will suffer the most will be the poorest and the ones who did least to contribute to the problem. As I see it, anyone who claims to follow in the steps of Jesus cannot ignore the problem and should not claim God's omnipotence as the excuse for inaction.

Our children are all happily married, and while none of them are regular churchgoers, they are kind and generous people. We also love our grandchildren to bits, and we worry a lot about the world they will inherit.

I always used to say that I wanted to go into my old age as a trouble-maker and, God willing, that may yet happen. Hopefully, it will be with Dave by my side, with the wonderful friends with whom we have shared so much of this journey, and the great sense of community we have enjoyed at TUC for nearly 40 years.

Faith stories from women in the pews

Life is a journey with a destination – an adventure with God

Mary M's story

Our God is weaving His story into each of our lives and through our lives to others. We may often only see the under-side and focus on the mess and knots in our lives and miss the beauty of the front of the tapestry as God transforms us to reflect who He is to the world. It is good to reflect and see what story God is weaving into our lives and ask ourselves the question: 'What's the point of life?" The Lord has shown me over and over again that He is using the circumstances of my life to mould me into the person I am today. He is in the business of moulding us into the people He has made us to be. This is one of my favourite verses from Jeremiah 29: 11-13

> For surely I know the plans I have for you, says the Lord, plans for your welfare and not for harm, to give you a future with hope. Then when you call upon me and come and pray to me, I will hear you. 1When you search for me, you will find me; if you seek me with all your heart.

As I grew up, I was aware of God's presence and at the age of twelve, I met Jesus personally, with an overwhelming experience of the Holy Spirit. This made God very real to me through my teen years. I knew Jesus as a companion which, in hindsight, was so important. I grew up in a fairly strict household. I was an only child and so often felt alone and had little fellowship. From a young age, I had the desire to teach. Looking back, I see the highlights of my teen years as teaching Sunday School, lifesaving and equipping girls in my patrol to pass their tests in Girl Guides. Through these years, I knew God's hand on my life, leading me as I made decisions on my course of study (to be a high school science teacher) and marriage.

In my mid-twenties, God placed me in His school of trust. Life was going well. I was happily married for four years and everything seemed to be going as planned. We had been overseas to see my father's family and I had become pregnant as planned. However, there were problems and the baby died at about 18 weeks in utero. Looking back, God put me in a place where I couldn't be in control so I could learn to put Him in control. Yes, He is in control of life and death. I could do nothing but trust Him. Over the next 3 years of waiting to carry a pregnancy full term, He taught me many things that strengthened the foundations of my relationship with Him. These included waiting on Him (Psalm 46:10), praising God in all circumstances (1Thesselonians 5:16-18), trusting in Him and His promises and God being our healer.

I remember clearly one night, after coming home from hospital tests, being full of desperation and fear that we would never have a family. I fell on my knees and asked what part of His word to read and Ephesians 3 came to mind and it was the last two verses that appeared in bold type:

*Now to him who is **able to do immeasurably more than all we ask or imagine**, according to his power that is at work within us, 21 to him be glory in the church and in Christ Jesus throughout all generations, for ever and ever! Amen.*
Ephesians 3: 20,21 (NIV)

Wonderful! The Holy Spirit poured joy and peace into my heart and I knew I could trust Him. He could do far more than I could imagine. I was learning to walk by faith not by sight.

The Lord continued to encourage me   Psalm 128:1-3 (NIV)

Blessed are all who fear the LORD, who walk in his ways. You will eat the fruit of your labour; blessings and prosperity will be yours. Your wife will be like a fruitful vine within your house; your sons will be like olive shoots around your table.

He gave this same verse to a friend 6 months later who passed it onto me. I was learning to take hold of His promises. I had to trust Him. He was the Giver of life. Finally, I felt God saying for me to give up work and I did. I fell pregnant and stayed pregnant this time. We were blessed with a beautiful son, followed by two beautiful daughters in the space of three and a quarter years. What joy and blessings!

Over this long time of waiting, I questioned: Why wasn't God healing me? In my search to understand, my husband and I studied a lot about God's healing, and this opened the door for us to be involved in healing and deliverance ministry later on. I struggled with the thought "I'm not good enough." What have I done wrong that God won't heal? What do I have to do to be healed?

Healing happened in many layers. One of the life changing things God revealed was how I see myself. God showed me that He doesn't make junk and He began to heal me emotionally. He showed me that I was a worthwhile person, not because of what I did but because of who I am. I realise now how important it is to see ourselves as God sees us. How we see ourselves influences how we relate to God and to others. For me as a young Mum, my biggest testing ground was my family. It was my reaction that counted in the unexpected dramas and hurdles that could be so frustrating. It seemed that often the little things caught me unawares as they built on each other. Over the years, I have learnt to pray first, then respond and correct instead of reacting and then praying. What a privilege to be a wife and mother! As the children were growing up, I could see that God put us in families to sand us down, to make us like a precious stone, crystal clear and finely honed, life of Jesus shining through, giving glory back to Him.

All I had to do was let go and let God love me, restore me and put my trust in Him. Easy to say but in reality, it's a process - it's a journey of discovery. As I continued my adventure with Jesus, I was aware that there was more- more to following Jesus. God revealed more of His heart and I longed to more fully embrace His desires and plans. Knowing the Father's heart brought a deeper sense of acceptance, security and new awareness of the depth of His amazing love.

As I choose to declare Jesus as Lord, I learnt to let go and allow His Holy Spirit to work bringing restoration and healing. I realise we each have a daily choice to allow His Truth to set us free (John 8:31-32) to be who He calls us to be. We can choose to bow to our brokenness or bow to the Risen King in our brokenness. As I took God at His Word, I saw many set free through prayer ministry.

This was a wonderful season in my life as the Lord nurtured my children in the faith and opened doors to opportunities in ministry particularly in the church and school. It was a season in learning to walk more intimately with Jesus. The Holy Spirit was teaching me to obey the prompting of His Spirit and walk in freedom. My identity is not a matter of who I am but whose I am. When Jesus is the centre, then life is about Him, it is not about me. That is so freeing. 'Christ in you, the hope of glory' Colossians 1:26-28

I had the opportunity to study the Bethel course, a biblical overview over 42 weeks and later to teach it. It was life changing to see the bible as God's Big Story- His Story and so appreciate each part in His big picture. The theme: 'Blessed to be a blessing,' hich is one of the threads through the entire bible from Genesis 12, became one of my life verses. Yes, we are blessed to be a blessing. There was such joy in serving as I used the gifts God had given me and I saw transformed lives as He worked in and through me. There were great opportunities to speak truth, life and encouragement in the lives of young leaders and particularly women.

Then came a season of shattered dreams. My marriage of thirty years ended in divorce. I was overcome with grief, disappointment, rejection, and shame. I felt like I was looking into a black hole and all seemed stripped away. In this rocky time in my life, I struggled to keep focus on God and believe the truth about myself. As I read a psalm a day, sometimes the same psalm for three days, He brought His word alive by His Spirit. I eclared this over my life as I went to work.

> *The LORD is my rock, my fortress and my deliverer;*
> *my God is my rock, in whom I take refuge.*
> *He is my shield and the horn of my salvation, my stronghold.*
> *I call to the LORD, who is worthy of praise.*
>   Psalm 18:2-3a (NIV)

God spoke to me words of encouragement as I rested in Him: 'just as I knit you together in your mother's womb so I knit you together inside.'(Psalm 139) He took my empty shell and began to restore my emotions and fill me up inside. Relationships with other Christians are always vital in our walk with Jesus. In this season, it was such a gift to have believers around me who could encourage and point me to the truth. God refocused me: 'Turn your eyes to Me. Life is not about you, It's about Me and My kingdom.' He opened up doors and began to show me new possibilities. He reminded me of my desire to be involved in missions from my teenage years. Now He gave me the opportunity to go on school mission trips to stir that desire in my heart.

God was in the business of restoration as He led me through opportunities to speak life and truth into students' lives, to demonstrate God's love and grace in teaching, pastoral care and welfare and training student leaders in peer leading, ISCF and school mission teams. It was wonderful to have the freedom to facilitate students to step out in faith and develop the gifts God had given them. I had the privilege to travel with school mission teams to the west for seven years and to Uganda on four occasions. Each time, I experienced how the Lord works in amazing ways, "far beyond what we can imagine" cross-culturally and in the lives of our students. He gave me more promises that sustained me on the journey of healing and restoration. On the second trip to the west, in the desert, He gave me Hosea 2:14-15 (NIV.)

> *Therefore I am now going to allure her;*
>   *I will lead her into the wilderness*
>   *and speak tenderly to her.*
> *There I will give her back her vineyards,*
>   *and will make the Valley of Achor a door of hope.*
> *There she will respond[c] as in the days of her youth,*
>   *as in the day she came up out of Egypt.*

What a promise of restoration which he emphasised by giving these verses twice more to friends for me. After a number of years, the winter passed and Spring came in its fullness in many ways.

> *My beloved spoke and said to me,*
>   *"Arise, my darling,*
>   *my beautiful one, come with me.*
> *See! The winter is past;*

the rains are over and gone.
Flowers appear on the earth;
the season of singing has come,
the cooing of doves is heard in our land.
The fig tree forms its early fruit;
the blossoming vines spread their fragrance.
Arise, come, my darling;
my beautiful one, come with me.
    Song of Songs 2:10-13 (NIV)

However, there were more challenges ahead. About 12 years ago, new uncertainties in life rocked my serenity. Something was radically wrong. Tests, scans and about six weeks of travelling in what seemed a dark tunnel before a diagnosis came, caused me to press into God and try to keep fear to a minimum. You see, I had already had a brush with cancer eight years before with a breast lump and certainly did not want to go down that track again. Finally, what a relief to know at last. It was Non-Hodgkin Lymphoma. Yes, cancer but one with a cure rate at a high percentage but now came the abhorrence of putting poisons in my body. That's just not for me!

All through the waiting and not knowing time I had cried out to God. I felt His Presence pour over me and yet He had not miraculously healed me. I don't often ask why – this time I did. Why do I have to go through all this? Why not just heal me? I said to myself: I've been in the school of trust before so I must be such a slow learner. God reprimanded me: Do not judge yourself as the world does and reminded me of some of the words given to me earlier.

I shall not die but shall live and shall recount the deeds of the Lord.
    Psalm 118:17

I took hold of that promise through the darkness and continued to press into God. I wrote in my journal: 'Your grace is enough for me. May I be so filled with your love that this would replace my fear.' This poem out of a book I was given "Just enough light" by Stormie Omartian meant a lot to me in these early weeks.

Faith stories from women in the pews

Sometimes only the step I'm on,
or the next one ahead,
is all that is illuminated for me.
God gives just the amount of light I need
for the exact moment I need it.
At those times I walk in surrender to faith,
unable to see the future
and not fully comprehending the past.
And because it is God who has given me what light I have,
I know I must reject the fear and
doubt that threatens to overtake me.
I must determine to be content where I am,
and allow God to get me where I need to go.
I walk forward,
one step at a time,
fully trusting that
the light God sheds
is absolutely sufficient.

Our God is so faithful. Each day God met me where I was. As I started treatment, God spoke clearly to me in Psalm 3 and reminded me that He is my shield and protector. He is my glory and the lifter of my head. Earlier that morning as I lay in bed, around four o'clock, I sensed the Lord say:

Look at Me
Look at my eyes, see how much I watch over you
Look at the cross, see how much I love you
Look at Me
I hold you in the palm of My hand
Look at Me

Wow. I lay there wrapped in his love and protection. In the morning, I realised that He was trying to refocus me to fix my eyes on Him and not my circumstances. I sensed as I went for treatment I went with the protection of the shield of His love. A scripture I read a couple of days before my hair was due to fall out. Proverbs 4: 9 "He will give you a garland to grace your head and present you with a glorious crown."

Wow! God had that covered too. I felt God saying as you lose your hair, do not feel naked and ashamed. I will crown you with wisdom; I will give you a garland of grace for your head.

I knew that God wanted to teach me more, to reveal to me more and I did not want to miss out on what He was doing. However, it felt like all was stripped away. It was only God and me. I cried out to the Lord. Help me to keep my focus on you. Help me to see you as my shepherd, my lover, my all in all. Help me to lean on you, to learn of you, to move into a new place with you where Your presence is so real in my life that other lives are touched and healed.

I remember intentionally having to stop sliding down the hopeless path and turn my focus to God and His perspective. Seeing everything through the lens of God's goodness helped claim victory in the mind. He was calling me to celebrate this glorious opportunity for revelation of the character of God, to see this season as an opportunity to know Him in a way I have longed to know Him

I remember making a choice: Yes, I can accept where I am and I also knew as I accepted the challenge, I accepted heaven's provision to get through the challenge. I could believe God's heart was overwhelmingly full towards me and my heart began to sing. Thanksgiving from the heart agrees with heaven by acknowledging the truth that our lives are a gift from God and that He is sovereign over all.

Yes, He was showing me things I knew but now I really knew. God wanted to grow me in confidence in who He is and to trust that He is in control, regardless of how things seemed. Experience is how we encounter truth. I was to relax in His goodness and His love. I could stand in the place of refreshing with a new dimension of His Presence, being transformed, so that I can carry His kingdom more intensely in my heart. It's about His presence and His nature. It's not about me but about God and His kingdom.

Now, I was waiting in a very different place. I had stopped. I had ceased to strive. Psalm 27 encouraged me in waiting, worship, and trusting God's goodness. Waiting on God is such a key in this journey:

> *Wait for the Lord;*
> *be strong and take heart*
> *and wait for the Lord.*
>   Psalm 27:13-14 (NIV)

Waiting on God is like 'rest that pursues', with a heart after God. This time with Him is vital to experience His love, being renewed in His Presence. It's about delighting in the Lord, seeking His face and hearing His heartbeat. This is where He plants His desires (Psalm 37:4) and shows us more of our assignments as we are called to continue the mission of Jesus (Luke 4:18-19). Yes, God is my King and He wants me to be in His throne room lavishing His love on me, revealing His wisdom, His thoughts and ways. (Acts 17:28)

Yes, it was a journey of surrender. This led to a new joy and a new clarity filled my mind. Whatever the cause, God takes charge of the situation. He allows it for my good and his glory. Through confession of my attitude, I knew a new liberation to celebrate His goodness and His faithfulness and the opportunities he has given me. He is with me each step.

However, there was another very real battle going on. As someone put it, there is a civil war happening in your body so pray: Your kingdom come. Let all the cells align with the kingdom of life. I put myself to bed each night in His river of healing- such peace and comfort flowed. I know that I was carried in prayer, sustaining by His Presence, encouraged by His word and encouraged greatly by the words and kindness of my brothers and sisters in God's family. It's about living as people of courage, holding on to His promises and speaking His life into all our relationships and circumstances. God was teaching me again to take time out to spend time with Him, enjoying His presence, coming with no agenda except to be in His presence. It was about resting in Jesus and waiting on Him.

This became a beautiful healing journey where I saw my priorities line up with His and my heart was beating more in rhythm with His heart. It is a journey of grace. I sensed His favour towards me – so undeserved. He is so faithful. He loves me and knows every little thing about me. He knows my next steps. He knows intimately my fears and concerns. He is my healer, my comfort and strength. He will refresh, renew and empower me as we wait in His Presence. He renews my strength. (Isaiah 40:31)

Again, six years later, I was living life to the full when I was struck again by the dreaded message: 'Good, you are back in Australia and your routine mammogram looks suspicious.' I could not believe it as I felt so good and had just returned from teacher training in Myanmar. Reality hit quickly and I was on the journey of treatment again. Again, God was so faithful and gave me the strength to cope, the comfort I needed and the courage to have faith that He would bring me through. He reminded me of the things he had shown me in the last journey including this verse: 'I shall not die but shall live and shall declare His works and recount the works of the Lord' (Psalm118:17.) It was a season to rest in Him, to commune with Jesus and I remember some special times with family and friends and being able to encourage them as they encouraged me. I remember the power of celebrating the steps of treatment and giving thanks to God each step of the journey, not because of how I felt but because of who He is. As He restored me, I felt a renewed passion to live life to the full and make the most of every opportunity as he continued to open doors.

I love seeing life as an adventure. It is about running the race God has planned for us, as our lives are part of His story. Each day I sense Him saying "Come to Me" "Fix your eyes on Me" (Hebrews12:2.) It can be a wakeup call: What am I focusing on?

Journeying through the challenges, certainly clarified who I am and whose I am and His priorities. Yes, I am the King's child, with a kingdom purpose, a planting of the Lord for the display of His splendour. (Isaiah 61) How I longed to make a difference but I knew it started in me. I needed to be intentional as I choose to keep Jesus at the centre of my life. I became very aware that I needed to position myself and 'be still in Him', to listen, let His love and His Spirit so fill me that I was available for Him. As He transformed me, He gave me the transforming message of the gospel for others, so as to bring heaven to earth, as we pray: Your kingdom come on earth as it is in heaven.

God uses everything in our lives to prepare us for the next steps.

As I retired from teaching, God used my twenty years' experience in Christian education and my training with New Hope International, to open opportunities to be involved in teacher training overseas. This is about equipping local teachers in Christian Education, firstly looking at establishing a Christ -centred, bible -based, Spirit -led, God fearing learning community and then applying this to teaching methods, a different way of teaching and learning which we seek to model as we journey through the concepts.

I thank God for the opportunities to be in partnership with Him in the lives of people in Myanmar and Nepal with "Transform the Nations" and a few years ago in Uganda and Bangladesh with New Hope International. He brings me right out of my comfort zone and to be ready for whatever. This helps me focus to seek God's agenda, and to be flexible as we come to serve the people. It has been so encouraging to see lives changed, teachers come to know Jesus, or to know Him more and His ways, teachers to see their students differently, made in God's image and gifted by Christ. They experience community during the course and want to take this back to their classroom or school. I remember one teacher writing in her feedback: "Thank you for introducing me to the master teacher, Jesus."

These cross-cultural opportunities emphasised for me the importance of seeing life and people through God's eyes and of working together in a Christ-centred, bible-based, Spirit-led community. This is a community which reflects the nature and character of God with a balance of love, justice and walking humbly with Him. (Micah 6:8) The heart of the gospel is all about love: Love God and love people. It is about establishing a culture of honour, choosing to forgive and not take offense and 'speaking the truth in love' (Ephesians 4:15), that is being 'Jesus with skin on'. This is loving as Jesus loves us. "Listening is the rarest form of love." How does anyone know they are loved if they are not listened to?

Again and again, I have seen the power of God transforming lives by His love and kindness, here and overseas. We offer our 'little' and He multiplies it. That is the currency of His kingdom. The cross is central to all of life as we take hold of the victory Jesus has won. The cross is also a good illustration of focusing us in our listening. The vertical represents our relationship with God the Father, Son and Holy Spirit and reminds us to listen to the promptings of the Holy Spirit. The horizontal highlights the importance of community, listening to the people around us. God showed me clearly that the strength of the community depends on the strength of the vertical. How important it is to spend time in His Presence so we can know Him, be refreshed and saturated by His love so that others will see Him in us and thirst for the truth. 'Listen Listen Love Love' is a good motto for life (which I first heard at the Kairos Outside) and very applicable in pastoral care.

God is continuing to grow my faith in Him. I am learning to walk by faith, not by sight. (2 Corinthians 5:7) As I pray and seek His heart: Lord, let my heart break with what breaks yours, I sense His desires, pain and longings. In intimacy, my heart beats with His heart, I see more from God's view and sense the prompting of His Holy Spirit. Nothing is impossible with Him. He is our God of restoration, turning darkness to light, death to life and there's always more. This verse I have seen in most of my life experiences:

"Now to him who is able to do immeasurably more than all we ask or imagine, according to his power that is at work within us, to him be glory in the church and in Christ Jesus throughout all generations, for ever and ever! Amen." (Ephesians 3:20-21)

God invites us to participate in the story that He is weaving into each of our lives. Isn't it wonderful to know we are all on a journey – the journey of life- but it is more than just a journey – it is an exciting, liberating adventure with the King of Kings and Lord of Lords.

What a destination!

Faith stories from women in the pews

When God seems close to me

Robyn W's story

I gave my heart and my life to the Lord Jesus Christ the day after my thirtieth birthday. Before I wanted Jesus in my life, I remember reading the poem 'Footprints' at a friend's house. The words of the poem gave me an amazing sense of God's love, although the reality of God's love and the free gift of salvation was something that came a couple of years later.

My traditional church background gave me an anonymous understanding of God. It was like I knew God existed, but I didn't know who God was. Mid 1990 a story emerged about the author of 'Footprints'. Later someone gave me a copy of the poem complete with the author's name. It was the first time I had seen her name attached to the poem since reading her story. She was no longer anonymous. It was a bit like that for me with God. And then God was no longer anonymous. He was a real person, someone I speak to, someone who listens to me, someone who answers prayers.

The times when God feels the closest are the times when I recognise that no matter how smart I think I am, His ways are always better. There is a freedom in this that could not be imagined. As He waits for me to be still and to listen to His words, I find a peace which does pass beyond human understanding. Revelation comes from knowing God has spoken a rhema word to me, that is, spoken directly into my heart.

There are days when I hear His heartbeat and I am able to respond.

Those are the days when God seems closer to me.

I will be with you

Helen E's story

Helen recently turned 100 and some months ago she was interviewed about her faith for a women's gathering. Helen was born in Madras and when asked about her faith beginnings she recalled that when she was a little girl every morning, she had to kneel with her Dutch grandfather at his bedside for morning prayers. Her grandfather was everything to her because her father, who was British walked out on the family when she was a child. Her mother had to go to work and her aunt looked after the children, doing so much for them. Helen said her aunt talked about the Lord and she taught the children to pray. Helen was very grateful to God saying her Dutch grandfather was very special and an example of our Heavenly Father.

Helen remembers she and her sister going with their grandfather to church every Sunday, morning and evening. They would be sitting under the pulpit and her sister would fall asleep. Their grandfather wanted them to tell him something about the sermon. He wanted to understand the 'gist' of it, so they couldn't fall asleep and had to stay attentive and listen. Helen recalls that her sister would fall asleep and she would ask Helen to tell her what the sermon was about.

Helen migrated to Brisbane in 1968 shortly after her daughter Dorothy and husband came to Australia. Within a year she was teaching at Indooroopilly Primary School where she taught for many years. Helen had a very supportive church family in Brisbane and moved to Canberra twenty years ago to be closer to her daughters and grandchildren. She became involved in Tuggeranong Uniting Church, participating in worship services and leading a seniors bible study group.

When asked about challenges to her faith over the years Helen said that she never had any doubts. She recounted a story about when she was preaching an hour away from Madras and suddenly the lights failed but she continued to preach and afterwards many people said that they had

Faith stories from women in the pews

heard every word.

When asked about what advice she would give younger women on their faith journey Helen said if you set a good example then there will be times when your friends will come with you to church. She also suggested that in whatever you are doing persist, be prepared to do something and listen to God's voice.

Helen's special verse to encourage others is Isaiah 43:2

> *When you pass through the waters, I will be with you*
> *When you pass through the rivers*
> *They will not sweep over you*
> *When you walk through the fire*
> *The flames will not set you ablaze*
> *For I am the Lord your God*
> *The Holy one of Israel, your Saviour.*

My journey, so far –
Mary H's story

I was introduced to my faith as a child and brought up on a family farm in mid-north South Australia, the second of 4 children. Our farm was situated some 16 km from each of the towns of Bute and Port Broughton in a district with a strong Methodist heritage and several ongoing Methodist congregations. Our local church, Wiltunga, was a small, isolated, stone-built church that was on the corner of a crossroad of the main road and local road approximately 10 km from our farm. Up to 16 families worshipped at the church. Alongside the church was a hall where Sunday school and church social activities were held. Our little church was part of a rural country circuit with the minister, based in Bute, servicing several rural congregations across a wide area of the mid-north of SA. After church, the members had many a long conversation with each other before eventually returning to their homes. Due to the isolation of farming life and cost/limited telephone this was as important for them both from a spiritual and social perspective.

I have memories of dressing in our "best clothes" to attend Sunday school, held to coincide with the church service. In addition to services and Sunday School, there were bring and share evening meals held regularly. In the cooler months there was often a bonfire that coincided with a meal. Different church calendars events were celebrated. e.g. Harvest thanksgiving, Sunday school anniversaries with children singing to the adults and the award of prizes to the children for the diligence in their Sunday school work.

My life changed drastically when I was 9 with the death of my mother from cancer after a short period of illness. This left my father with four children aged 12 and under with the youngest approaching five. Our home life from that day forward included a housekeeper. Our housekeeper for the next nine years, known as Aunt Min, was a mature aged spinster with an Anglican background. Efforts were made to maintain household routine (for a while) which required Aunt Min to learn to drive to allow her to take us to the Sunday school. As a good Anglican she wanted to make sure her charges were brought up with a relationship to church. Her driving occasionally stretched to the nearer towns – she was clearly not confident or comfortable driving.

As I entered my teenage years, I attended RAYS (a Methodist girl's youth group) this was held in the town of Bute. Aunt Min would drive my elder sister and me a few km down the road to a neighbour who was a leader of the RAYS. Our involvement led to confirmation class and then being confirmed in the Methodist church.

On completing school, I left the district to commence nurse training in Adelaide, some 160 km from the farm. Shift work, living in the nurses' home and study was not conducive to being involved with any church or group. Aunt Min, who continued to maintain the 'home' for my father and younger brother and sister, died from an aneurysm when I had been a trainee nurse for four months.

While I was still in training as a registered nurse in Adelaide, I met my husband, Chris. In our first year together, he joined the RAAF which set the stage for a range of different challenges. We were married in the Methodist Church at Wiltunga and I started an interesting life journey as the spouse of a serving member including many periods of separation and solo child rearing ranging from days, through weeks to months.

I had little involvement with church for a couple of years being newly married, continuing nursing studies, shift work and juggling demands of Chris's military life, his study and starting a family. When our first son was born, Chris was notified of a posting to Penang in Malaysia. We spent two and a half years in Penang and started to attend church again. It was quite a different experience from Wiltunga. We attended the Protestant RAAF service that was conducted on alternate Sundays by the Anglican or Presbyterian chaplains at a local school. This meant that we had a service in English but different influences – one week Anglican the next Presbyterian. As we were part of the military contingent that was in Penang at the time it was also a way of getting to know other fellow members who had a Christian faith. The Uniting Church in Australia came into being while we were in Penang.

This period exposed me to diverse spiritual beliefs and religious practices. Our neighbours included Malay Muslim and Chinese Buddhists and Taoists. While Malaysia has a secular constitution, some areas were strongly focussed on Sharia practices including having religious police to enforce precepts on the faithful.

At the end of our posting, we returned to Adelaide, now with two children. The challenges of Chris's work including his deployments and dealing with two infant boys plus reconnecting with family left little time for organised religion. Some 2 years later we were posted to Melbourne where we had no family and knew absolutely no one. Early in our time in Melbourne, as my twenty ninth birthday approached, my father died suddenly while in hospital recovering from surgery. I was five months into my pregnancy with our third child at the time. Again, the Wiltunga church community came to the fore, and advised us that they would take care of the afternoon tea for my father's funeral service, leaving my siblings and me free to mourn our father's passing.

This generous action left a lasting imprint on me as I became aware that with a church community there are many layers. From the teaching of the scriptures through to the invaluable unspoken support at a difficult time in one's life. Following my father's death, we engaged with the Newport Uniting Church for about a year. They were welcoming and forgiving of our older boys' antics and then the baby's occasional outbursts during services. Newport Uniting accepted our two younger sons into Christ's family through baptism.

We moved to our first 'own home' in Werribee in Victoria and became involved with the Uniting Church in Werribee. This provided us with social network with fellow parents with children of similar age, as well as our youngest child developing a strong grandparent type connection with a member of the congregation.

Life was progressing well, when again a posting occurred this time to Katherine in the Northern Territory. Again, we went seeking a church and community. The demography of Katherine was of a younger age group. Although we were living in the town of Katherine, we started by attending the Protestant (Anglican) service on the RAAF base. We had been in town about four months when the great Christmas exodus of families south to avoid the wet season and share Christmas with families took place. The small worship community was very inclusive of the 'orphan' families, including us, who were left behind.

We ended up worshipping with a congregation that was run by a Southern Baptist missionary minister and his wife from America. We met in the high school which was walking distance from our home. It was an interesting time. Music was provided by a whoever was available from members of the congregation through to passing tourists who could play the piano with the songs being whatever the musician of the day could play.

We were varied in age and denomination and included the local Salvation Army captain and wife. There was a small youth group that our two older boys attended. We were involved in a bible study group of people who were of similar age and were from different parts of Australia so there was a lot of interesting discussion. Again, it enabled us to connect with the local community and it allowed us to be our own identity without being identified by a military rank or position.

At the end of the posting cycle, we were posted to Canberra (again we knew no one).

We ended up living in southern Canberra with the closest church being Tuggeranong Uniting Church. We attended and found the church to be a vibrant active church. We were made welcome. We became involved with the church as it was a way to get to know people of our own age group knowing that with church teaching their values would be like ours. This resulted in us being involved with a small group that is still active. Through the ensuing years the small group has been invaluable with providing support as we all struggled at times with growing children and the challenges that involves through to work and life issues. We have evolved from having coffee and desert nights with children, to soup evenings, a Christmas meal annually, to having themed meals where we each bring part of the meal.

We had a posting back to our hometown of Adelaide some 11 years after arriving in Canberra. We became involved with a little church of

Greenwith Uniting close to where we lived. It was a small congregation of locals in an area where the urban sprawl had come to them. Consequently, it was in the throes of change as the surrounding area was experiencing a new housing growth and the congregation was testing the limits of its existing facilities. We returned to Canberra and the community we knew some 18 months later where we remain.

Reflecting on my journey, I have become aware of the lasting impact and importance the church community has had on me, particularly in time of trial and grief. Looking back, I could not discern any Road to Damascus moment that changed my beliefs, but rather realised that I had been steeped in the Christian community from an early age.

We all experience highs and lows in life. At times, I have felt very alone on this road, and I have struggled to make sense of my journey. My faith has sustained me throughout. I feel my willingness to be involved in opportunities to study and hear others' views and interpretations of the Bible has been the underpinning of my sustained faith over time. It is a comfort to have my faith to sustain and support me in my life.

Journeying in another culture
Maxine's story

All is change, woe and weal
Joy is sorrow's brother
Grief and gladness steal
Symbols of each other.
     Tennyson

The above encapsulates my life -lots of changes/adventures/blessings; interesting and exciting times, interspersed with some bad and sad times. Probably a lot like yours…

I will start from1976, when at 31, husband, James and our two children aged 11 and 10 went to live in Papua New Guinea. We became really interested in going when an ex-Beaufighter pilot comrade of my then father-in-law visited the family. He had a coffee plantation in the Highlands of PNG and suggested it would be a great enterprise for the whole family to take up. No one did that, but when an accountancy position was advertised, James applied (with no discussion with me!)

We'd also heard a lot about PNG through friends, and a cousin of James's, married to a Seventh Day Adventist pastor living in the Highlands. The heat from the tarmac when we arrived was overwhelming, but the bougainvillea everywhere was beautiful, and the anticipation of a very different lifestyle was enticing for us. Reality hit when we found that we didn't have a house to move into. Squatters had discovered the empty house, so had to be removed and the house cleaned up. Nothing was done because we had landed the day after Independence Day celebrations – things moved at a slower pace; true PNG style to which we had to adapt, along with the stifling heat and humidity.

There was, we found happily, a real sense of community. We moved into temporary lodgings in the 'city' area, and were mostly fed by the Personnel manager and wife, so they became firm friends. Their son was our son's age, and so Andrew was encouraged to join the Scouts. We were soon drawn in and befriended by the four other accountants who also worked for Steamships. (The other main company in PNG then was Burns Philp.) A sweet couple we'd met on the plane over 'adopted' our children as their grandchildren and moved to a house a few doors from us.

Our house faced east and west with no air conditioning and needed painting. We did have ceiling fans however. It was in ANGAU Drive, Boroko with Michael Somare's house further down the street. He moved about a year later into his "White House" in Waigani, an outer suburb, somewhat similar to our Embassy area in Canberra. Unfortunately, this meant we didn't have police walking regularly past our house after that.

We soon met our neighbours who'd just arrived back from a holiday in the UK where they'd unhappily experienced a heat wave. Olive asked me to which church I belonged, and I was able to inform her that not long beforehand I had been confirmed into the Anglican church. She was delighted to tell me that their family attended the little Anglican church in Boroko. So was the beginning of an amazingly close friendship which we still enjoy despite Olive living in Queensland!

Their three children were very close in ages to ours and many hours were spent in the respective back yards after school: the girls playing elastics, and the boys building jumps for their bikes, among other pursuits. They were often with the five children from the next house, and another lass from the house over the road also. Jenni and Olive's older daughter joined the Guides and also learnt ballet. Soon all the families got to know each other, and we shared many happy times; sometimes at the local Ela Beach, Variata Park in the hills, and other beautiful swimming spots. The local clubs provided outdoor movies and good, cheap food.

It seemed mostly both parents worked, but not so for three of us mums, sometimes more. We spent afternoons in one or another's house 'taking tea,' and the latest recipe we had made. Not that it was a lazy lifestyle: Olive and I were both asked to provide 'religious education' in some of the primary schools. It is in the requirements of education there (maybe still?) to have RE in the schools. Olive and I both played guitar well enough to accompany simple songs from "Hi God" and our favourite choruses which filled some of the time. Arch Books were great for the little ones too. Sometimes a young person from our church would join us. I particularly remember when one young lad had said he was coming to the house, but he was running late. I was cranky anyway for some reason; not really in the mood to be the upbeat Christian teacher I should be. On the way in the car, he started playing guitar and singing in his own language, and immediately I felt my heart change. He taught me that song in Hiri Motu and Pidgin so that I could sing along with other National children.

The International High School had us (and other 'teachers' from various churches) come in once per term for a half day of talking with the students. Very special times with great young adults where we tried to answer their questions honestly and directly.

We had booked our children into the Catholic primary school which had been recommended to us. I loved that the pupils were expected to go into the church next to the school to offer prayer for themselves and others before school. It was a good choice to send them there as it turned out. (Most National children went to T Schools which did not offer the higher standard of education).

Olive and I met on Monday mornings to meditate and pray. The little book "God Calling," by Two Listeners, and the Bible provided our inspiration for the day. They were very special times of providing strength and healing for us both, and hopefully we could encourage others in their day-to-day life. As it happens, two of the mums who attended our afternoon tea sessions came back to a faith when they moved back to Australia. They did confess that in their days in PNG they thought Olive and I were a little mad! Maybe God's love did overflow from us, despite us!

There was also a group of women who met from the various denominations for prayer and study. On one such day, one of them prayed specifically for me. I felt like I was lost in the warmth of love; and Jesus was blessing me in an incredible way. I am so blessed in so many ways, but

I felt humbled but strong from that moment. It was something I could describe as a transforming moment in my life.

Some of us passed the little book around by Merlin Carothers "Prison to Praise" which turned my attitude to any personal suffering I felt, to thankfulness, rather than holding onto the hurt, or feeling depressed. I binged on heaps of books by Christian writers, and we also listened to tapes from a minister in Canada – whose name escapes me, but I was thankful for his teachings, and the music too. It was a time of renewal and strengthening of my faith.

I loved our Church. It was a ninety percent National congregation, with a few dogs wandering in from time to time as well! Some would walk from the Six Mile settlement to come of a Sunday morning. (That's a six-mile walk!) The expats 'did church' like our Western church, complete with a choir. When our delightful Father Ray became our priest, he felt that the National people should be the leaders of worship, which seemed right to me in that we were in their country, and ultimately, they would take over the running of their church. The choir did not agree and left to go to the more 'high' church in the city which upset Father Ray, but it was the best thing to happen. From then on, with some help and encouragement, the younger Nationals provided music their style, and beautiful services. Ray had a real heart for the people, visiting the hospital and squatter settlements regularly, extending himself so much that he protracted hepatitis which laid him low for some time.

The Anglican Church was established in the Popondetta/Oro Bay region where they built a hospital. This is where the other end of the Kokoda Trail ends. Our Bishop, and Archbishop was David Hand who was engaged to a nurse there before the Japanese landed. She and another nurse were captured by the Japanese, imprisoned and finally killed. Bishop David never married. The building where they were imprisoned is still there, and around it are beautiful huge plane trees. The Anglicans built Martyrs School, and when Olive and I visited there, the children were all seated around outside singing – it was as I imagine heaven might be like.

James did not attend church or profess to any faith but really enjoyed all

Faith stories from women in the pews

our gatherings with Father Ray, Bishop David, members of the congregation who all became close friends.

I was asked to be godparent to a little National girl who is now a mother and employed by Air Nuiguini, and we are in contact still, also godparent to three children of another family; the father of whom played Aussie Rules with James. We were in contact for many years, but sadly not now.

Andrew attended the local Baptist church as he made friends with lads from there. One of them is still his best friend – 40 plus years later! Jenni attended Boroko Anglican Church with me and made the decision to be confirmed by Father Ray.

Archbishop Donald Coggins and his wife visited from the UK when there was a spectacular sing-sing in full traditional costume by the Nationals. They love to perform for hours but it was extremely hot for the visitors, and eventually the priest in charge had to tell them it was enough! Frangipani absolutely filled our little church, and there were various musicians. In the evening there was a huge gathering of people and leaders from all the Christian churches in Port Moresby at the largest sporting area. I found that there was more 'overlapping' of the denominations in PNG than in Australia. For instance, the Missionary Aviation Fellowship providing flights for missionaries and those needing medical transport is financed by all the church bodies.

Mother Teresa (so tiny!) also visited, and it was such a privilege to meet and listen to her.

Queen Elizabeth and Prince Phillip provided another highlight and celebration.

After three years of feeling very blessed in this place, things were changing. Lawlessness was present and becoming worse. People from other parts of PNG were coming into Moresby with the hope of gaining work, but there is a limit to the more menial jobs, and these people were mostly illiterate, or with no trade they could use in the city. The Nationals have this "Wantok' (speak the same language) obligation in that if a person was from their area, then they had to be provided with hospitality. They were obliged to support and share everything, but the problem was that the city dwellers were battling to support themselves, let alone support others. Squatter settlements were growing, groups of "rascal gangs" would fill the roadway creating unrest with break ins. In fact, our clothesline was a target from even our house help's friends; if there was something that they needed, for example a towel, then it was considered theirs!

One Sunday afternoon after James had left to go to Aussie Rules, and after a church service that morning when Father Ray exhorted us to be sure to treat the National people with respect and patience, I popped out to the front veranda because the dog was barking. There was a National there who said he needed a check cashed. I apologised explaining I couldn't do that, but he kept talking. The dog was barking so I told him to lie down and be quiet. (Not the thing to do when we bought him as a guard dog!) I opened the veranda gate to allow the neighbour's lass to go out and the man took the opportunity to lunge up and hold me around the throat from behind. I knew that Jenni was inside and tried to yell for her to get help and she eventually heard and raced out the back door to the neighbours – after picking up a rock and aiming at the guy – it missed. The man was trying to drag me inside but I was strong enough to resist. A car came along the road, so he let go and ran down the side road which leads to the hospital. He would know that he could easily get lost in the crowd there. University students were in the car, and they tried to chase him up as they told me that he would come back so as not to lose face. My dear neighbour came racing in with a spade, but I wouldn't let him chase the attacker as I didn't want him hurt. I took a while to get over the shock of it all, and I had to reassure Father Ray that he wasn't at fault with his sermon!

The man did come back. Once again, the gate was open with James's head stuck in the car engine, so he didn't notice the unwelcome visitor. I tried to scream out from the kitchen just as the man was going to go up the stairs, but thankfully James saw him and sent him going. I had said to James that the day a 10-foot, barbed wire topped fence was erected around the house, would be the day that we would leave. That was prophetic, as that is what happened: We had spent a week at Rabaul having an interesting and enjoyable holiday. On arriving back at the house, the workmen had started the fence, and we booked our flights back to Australia the following day.

The day I wrote this faith story, (and a whole lot more which I could not burden you with) was the birthdate of both of my dear children. My daughter took her life nearly eight years ago. I grieve and always will, but this, my hardest lesson, has made me take stock of who I am and what I want to be. I am thankful for all that life has thrown at me, and I'm so thankful that Jenni has blessed me during her life and even now.

Luke 10:27 says, "You shall love the Lord your God with all your heart, and with all your soul, and with all your strength, and with all your mind; and your neighbour as yourself." Beatrice Bruteau interprets (paraphrased) Heart as affectivity, soul as imagination, strength as will, and mind as intellect. I hope I can continue utilising all those bodily gifts, though I am very much lacking in godly traits – very much a 'work in progress' - catching myself saying what I shouldn't, not caring enough or listening enough. Thank God I don't have to earn a place in God's heart as He is full of grace and love.

On a journey
Margaret's story

Being on a journey is a favourite motif for life, particularly in literature. It occurs many times in the Biblical narrative. The story of Abram and Sarai (later to be called Abraham and Sarah) leaving their settled life to follow a call from God to an unknown destination and new identities is one of my favourites. Their journey into the unknown began when they were quite old and should have been retiring or at least preparing for it.

So it was for me. At the age of 55 – not quite as old as Sarai and Abraham - I took my first steps into the unknown, on a journey that would see me become an ordained minister of the word in the Uniting Church.

Where did the journey start? The beginning was in my family home in the southern Sydney suburb of Caringbah. There, as the eldest of three girls, I learned about family life with its struggles, joys, and heartache. The sudden and tragic death of my youngest sister at seven years of age, scarred me deeply.

Our parents were typical Aussie battlers who had little but love, Christian values and hard work to offer their children. I remember a wonderful childhood. Through family outings and holidays, I grew to love the beach and the bush.

My father encouraged us all do our best at whatever we did. I inherited his love of literature and learning. Through Mum, who was a pianist, I grew to love classical music. Sport, especially hockey and squash in my teenage years, was also important. Most importantly, my mother encouraged her girls to think beyond the expectation of marriage and childbearing to be financially self-supporting, independent young women.

For our parents, Caringbah Methodist Church, just a short mile's walk mile down the road, was the centre of their lives. Not surprisingly, it became the centre of my life for the next 20 years of my life. As soon as we were old enough, my sisters and I were enrolled in Sunday School. At one stage there were nearly 200 children attending. Some classes had to be held outside which presented a problem when it rained - which was often!

We were the baby boomer generation. In the 1950s, Caringbah was a rapidly growing new suburb. These were the optimistic post war years and learning about the Christian faith was seen as vital to the life of young people. I remember fondly one of my Sunday School teachers- a small, very old, single woman (Miss Nelson, a daughter of the pioneering family in the Caringbah district) who, in her seventies, couldn't manage us rowdy children but loved us all anyway. She was a wonderful example of faithful dedication.

There were Sunday School anniversaries, that special time when my sisters and I always had a new dress and shoes to wear. We learned bible verses on little text cards and sat for Sunday School exams. In my teenage years I became a Sunday School teacher and discovered my love of teaching which led me to train as a primary school teacher. Youth group activities were our social outings, and many young couples went on to married life. Jobs were plentiful, life was good but few of my friends of those years remained in the church.

As a young adult I left Sydney to begin primary school teaching in Albury. There I met and married but after a couple of years, the marriage failed, leaving me with two young boys to care for. As life fell apart, I realised I was carrying a very heavy burden of guilt. I had been pregnant when I married and now my two boys had no father. My foundation in the faith had been quite conservative and did not help me in this crisis. It had given me a sense of belonging and purpose but somehow, I had the idea that being a faithful Christian meant you had to always be good and not make mistakes. The danger of straying off the narrow path was eternal damnation. I learned about the righteousness and judgement of God but somehow, the good news of unconditional love, the grace of God, had not reached me.

With my so-called Christian values in tatters, I returned to the family home and went back to teaching. Mum and dad were there for me and my little family, never condemning, only caring and loving. My mother suggested that I return to church which I did, somewhat nervously. Despite my misgivings, I soon found myself welcomed back into the local church as a Sunday School teacher and Sunday School superintendent – it was still a Methodist church in 1974.

Indulging my love of music, I joined the church choir. There I met Iain. We married in 1975 and made our first home in Caringbah. After the birth of our daughter Sandra, I suffered a deep, post-natal depression. During that very bleak period, my sense of guilt resurfaced and was almost suffocating. Over time, with the support of a loving husband, a supportive mother, caring friends and prayer, the depression slowly lifted.

As a married couple and young family, our involvement in the Caringbah Methodist Church continued and we were happy to become Uniting Church members in 1977 on the formation of the new church. Sandra was the first baby baptised in Caringbah Uniting Church. With the birth of our son, David in 1979, I was now the mother of four healthy children.

In every journey there are surprising twists and turns. One morning I was sitting in the lounge room reading Colossians in preparation for a women's Bible study. Suddenly it seemed as though a blind had been pulled open in my mind. The light of God's love and mercy came flooding into the dark corners of my consciousness. Judgement and guilt melted away in the brilliant light. All that could be seen was grace and divine love! The moment was so liberating, giving such a deep sense of peace and freedom, I felt like a new woman. It was my "born again" moment! My faith was no longer a burden but a joy.

The next stage of the journey began when we relocated from Caringbah to Canberra in 1981 by Iain's employer, the National Australia Bank. New experiences and companions came into our lives. Living first in Evatt and then Kaleen, we attended the North Belconnen Uniting Church but after a couple of years, for various reasons we connected up with the local Baptist Church where the younger children enjoyed Boys and Girls Brigades. To my surprise, I found myself leading adult Bible studies and small groups. In these congregations, the tiniest seeds of my call were planted.

In 1988, life began to change. Iain the left the bank and became the owner/operator of a small business. We bought our present home in Chisholm. Our two older sons had joined the work force. I was busy with relief teaching, tutoring, and managing the family. As we established ourselves in Chisholm, I felt the Spirit guiding us back to the Uniting Church.

We became members of Tuggeranong Uniting Church in the latter part of 1989. At that time, there were three distinctly different morning worship services and two ministers in placement - Reverend Tony Hooper and Reverend Joyce Scheitel.

There were now a few more surprises in my journey. First came a rethink of my understanding of scripture. The catalyst was the vital ministry of Joyce Scheitel. The problem for me, strange as it may seem, was a theological one. Joyce was a female minister! Her ministry was fruitful, and she was much loved. But doesn't the Bible say that women should be silent in church? It seems incredible to me now that I should have held such a literalist view of the Bible given my education, life experiences and serious reflection over the years. Incredible and hugely ironic!

Then early in 1990, Tony Hooper conducted a Covenant Service, a beautiful service carried over from our Methodist tradition.

> *I am no longer my own, but yours. Put me to what you will, rank me with whom you will;*
>
> *put me to doing, put me to suffering; let me be employed for you or laid aside for you;*
>
> *exalted for you or brought low for you; let me be full, let me be empty; let me have all things, let me have nothing; I freely and wholeheartedly yield all things to your pleasure and disposal. And now, glorious and blessed God, Father, Son and Holy Spirit, you are mine and I am yours, to the glory and praise of your name. Amen.*
>
>   (John Wesley)

The words came alive as I prayed them. It was as if God was using them to get my attention, especially the phrase "let me be laid aside for you." "What could that mean?" I wondered. To be "laid aside" seemed impossible for someone like me - always busy, always involved in something! But, "laid aside" it was to be.

For some reason, I felt that the restlessness I was experiencing would be settled by upgrading my teachers certificate to Bachelor of Education. So, I withdrew all my involvement in the life of the church to study. It is hard to describe the sense of futility and disappointment I experienced on completion of the course. I felt that it had all been a waste of time! I no longer wanted to be involved in school teaching. Imagine my surprise and relief, on discovering four years later, while exploring the educational requirements of the candidating process, a second degree was a necessary prerequisite for enrolling in the Bachelor of Theology degree course as a candidate for ministry in UCA! The study had not been a waste of time after all!

Back to 1992. With school teaching no longer of any interest, I began to wonder what was next. Again, the words of the Covenant Prayer came to mind. "Put me to what you will….". Study theology a friend suggested! Why not?

Taking up the challenge, I enrolled in the Batchelor of Theology course at St Mark's, Barton beginning with Biblical Studies. From the very first class, I had an overwhelming feeling that I was in the right place doing the right thing. It seemed that I was being set free to enjoy the Bible in a new way and to experience God in new understandings.

Suddenly, I was no longer "being laid aside." Leadership in the congregation became my life – eldership, working in the church office, learning about church administration and worship leading, becoming the Small Group Coordinator, joining a team providing weekly services in the UnitingCare Mirinjani Nursing Home, even occasionally preaching at the 9.30am service and more. All new and deeply satisfying experiences.

As this phase of my journey intensified, the idea of ordained ministry was raised by several people. I was unconvinced at first. The implications were mind-blowing - for Iain, our children and me. Yet the sense of being called became stronger and stronger. During my Emmaus Walk in 1997, I could no longer resist, deciding to test this sense of call by candidating for ordained Ministry of the Word in the UCA.

The actual journey for which I had unknowingly been preparing, began in earnest in 1999 when Iain and I relocated to United Theological College at North Parramatta (Sydney) to complete my degree in theology and begin the formation process.

As often happens when you begin a journey whether it be on a hike, in a caravan or go on a car trip, it doesn't take long to discover the 'stuff' that would have been better not taken. Leaving behind a fear of failure would have made the travelling easier. Even though all my children were young working adults with lives of their own, not worrying about them would also have helped.

But there was also plenty of good stuff. The best equipment I took was a strong marriage which was sorely tested as Iain and I moved into a single bedroom townhouse after living in a four-bedroom house. There we began the experience of role reversal – Iain learning to be the home manager, cook and general bottle washer while I studied; and me learning not to offer "helpful" advice from the side lines.

Life experience was another great piece of equipment to have. My ability to study, my love of learning and good health were also great assets. Discovering that my own brokenness through grief, divorce and depression would enable me to walk with others in similar circumstances, especially women, was a gift from God. We also took with us the love and encouragement of most of our church family, especially our small group, and our children. Yes, there were some who expressed the view that God does not call women into ordained ministry, especially a divorcee!

There were many new and challenging experiences over the next three years leading to ordination at Tuggeranong Uniting Church on 17 December 2000.

My life journey now merged with my journey as a Minister of the Word.

I served in two placements before retiring in 2011. One on the Mid North coast of NSW and the other in the Central West of NSW. Since retiring and returning to our home in Chisholm, there has been more than enough work as a supply minister plus involvement in the life of Tuggeranong Uniting Church, to keep me as active as I now choose to be and as age permits.

The words of Isaiah 43, spoken over me by the Tuggeranong Church Council back in 1997 were prophetic and encouraging:

> *Do not be afraid. I have called you by name. You are mine. Do not remember the former things or consider the things of old. I am about to do a new thing; now it springs forth, do you not see it?*

They remain inspirational as my journey in life, faith and service to God continues.

Faith stories from women in the pews

www.ingramcontent.com/pod-product-compliance
Lightning Source LLC
Chambersburg PA
CBHW051455290426
44109CB00016B/1764